Drinking the Mountain Stream

Milarepa and his lineage gurus: Marpa, Tilopa, and Naropa

Drinking
the
Mountain Stream

Songs of Tibet's Beloved Saint, Milarepa

Eighteen selections from the rare collection
Stories and Songs from the Oral Tradition of Jetsün Milarepa

Translated by Lama Kunga Rinpoche & Brian Cutillo

Illustrations by Amy Soderberg

Wisdom Publications • Boston

WISDOM PUBLICATIONS
361 Newbury Street
Boston, Massachusetts 02115
USA

First published by Lotsawa, P. O. Box 17127, Boulder, CO 80308
This revised edition 1995

Library of Congress Cataloging-in-Publication Data
Mi-la-ras-pa, 1040–1123.
    [Selections. English. 1995]
    Drinking the mountain stream : songs of Tibet's beloved saint, Milarepa : eighteen
selections from the rare collection : stories and songs from the oral tradition of Jetsün
Milarepa ; translated by Lama Kunga Rinpoche and Brian Cutillo.
        p.   cm.
    Originally published: New York : Lotsawa, 1978
    ISBN 0-86171-063-0 (alk. paper)
    1. Spiritual life—Buddhism.   I. Kunga, Rinpoche 1937–   . II. Cutillo, Brian.
    III. Title.
BQ7950.M552 1995
294.3'83—dc20   95-18671

ISBN 0 86171 063 0

00 99 98 97 96
  6 5 4 3 2

Cover illustration: In Tibet, sacred texts, called *pe-cha*, are traditionally regarded as the actual
teachings of the Buddha, and as such are treated with reverence. Texts are kept high above the ground
and carefully wrapped in cloth covers, called *pe-re*, to protect them from dust and damage.
Here, a brocade cloth covers a book of daily prayers.

Designed by: LJ·SAWLiT'

Illustrations by: Amy Soderberg

Typeset in Diacritic Garamond, Adobe Garamond
and Truesdell at Wisdom Publications by: Jason Fairchild

Wisdom Publications' books are printed on acid-free paper and meet the guidelines for permanence and
durability of the Committee on Production Guidelines for Book Longevity of the Council on Library Resources.

Printed in the United States of America.

All the water and drink you've consumed
Through beginningless time until now
Has failed to slake thirst or bring you contentment.
Drink therefore this stream
Of enlightenment mind, fortunate ones.

—*Milarepa*

Contents

Preface

by LAMA KUNGA RINPOCHE
formerly Thartse Shabthung of Ngor Monastery, Tibet

MILAREPA IS ONE OF THE MOST celebrated spiritual teachers of all time. He was not only an eminent leader of the Kagyupa lineage, but also a very important teacher for all schools of Tibetan Buddhism. He was a star of early Buddhism in Tibet, and a brilliant star of yoga that shines on the path of Dharma today. Certainly he was not a paranoid man who left society and hid in the corners of deep caves. In fact, he was an adventurer who reached the summit of the high mountain with a panoramic view of samsara (*saṁsāra*). He was a true warrior who succeeded in conquering the real enemy, thus becoming a savior of beings.

He was a man of three powers. His body was equivalent to the body of Vajrapāṇi, his voice was the voice of Mañjuśrī, and his hearing was the hearing of Avalokiteśvara. Milarepa was a healthy, vital man of matchless endurance in the search for liberation. His voice was beautiful and capable of rendering anything in spontaneous song, and with it he expressed the essence of the Buddha's Dharma in ways understandable to all types of listener. His hearing was as penetrating as Avalokiteśvara's, the compassionate bodhisattva the Tibetans call Chenrezi, who attends to the voices of all living beings.

There is a saying among the common people of Tibet, "In the forest the baboons and monkeys are most agile. In the barnyard the cows and sheep are most stupid. In the mountains Milarepa is the most skillful in meditation." As I said, Milarepa was a very illustrious yogi in Tibet, and perhaps the best known in the rest of the world. When his guru Marpa Lotsawa went to India to study with Nāropa, Nāropa said to him, "You should know that in the future you will have a disciple who will excel even his own teacher. The son is greater than the father, and the grandson will be greater than all of us." He then folded both hands together at his chest, bowed in the direction of Tibet, and saluted the future yogi Milarepa with this verse:

> I bow to that buddha
> Named "Mila Who Is Joy To Hear,"
> Shining like the sun on snow peaks
> In the dark gloom of the Land of Snows.

Milarepa sang many songs in his lifetime. It is said that most of them were stolen by the ḍākinīs. It seems that Mila was a popular teacher among nonhumans also! The particular collection of songs we have translated for this book has never been rendered into a western language before. We were very fortunate to have come across this rare and precious book and to have been able to translate it through the auspices of Lotsawa and Ewam Choden Center.

If the reader is expecting something like a magical and instantaneous reward from this book, I would say that it is rather difficult—do something else. This book is not just a collection of entertaining short stories. It should be read like a road map while traveling through the unfamiliar inner roads on the way to the central valley of the fully aware mind where you can peacefully camp out. It is not like tantalizing a child with the sight of plastic toys just out of reach. This is the real thing—like a child being nourished by a good mother. So read this book carefully with the alert attention of a traveler. However, everything will not be immediately understandable. When traveling by map and reaching an unfamiliar town one must stop and get detailed information of the locality that is not clear on the map. Similarly, the reader of this book should find assistance to get at the meaning of these songs, a special teacher who is skilled in this particular subject. The book, the reader, and the teacher together might produce something of value, something useful. It's good to read this kind of book, but studying it is better. And better yet is to extract its significance and apply it in practice.

I'm very grateful to my co-translator, Brian Cutillo, whose knowledge of Tibetan and the subjects of Buddhism and whose experience in translating Buddhist works have made this collaboration successful. I am grateful also to those who have helped in this work, particularly Vivian Sinder and James Wallace in the development and editing of *Drinking the Mountain Stream* as a book, Acarya Losang Jamspal for clarification of a number of points in my absence, and Nathan Swin for furnishing the Tibetan xylograph.

I sincerely wish that all readers of these songs of Milarepa find the inspiration to practice and ultimately realize the true meaning of human life. Thus this book is dedicated to the work of Ewam Chöden and to religious practitioners everywhere.

Drinking
the
Mountain Stream

Songs of Tibet's Beloved Saint, Milarepa

Introduction

Milarepa relates his first meditational experience to Marpa

Milarepa's World

THE INDIAN MASTER PHADAMPA SANGYE once told Jetsün Milarepa, "Your lineage is like a river stream—it will flow a long way." And it has, remaining vital and alive up to the present day. It's no coincidence that Milarepa's extemporaneous teachings in song are receiving attention now from the western world's practitioners, for our religious situation is much like that of Mila's time.

Until the advent of Buddhism in Tibet, the people were for the most part religiously naive, following a cult of elaborate shamanism. As Buddhism began to be assimilated through the teachings of representatives of many diverse schools, a process of evaluation, adaptation, and integration was begun, leaving in its wake a newly awakened religious consciousness. Likewise in the West, our religious traditions have been established for many centuries as a tacit acceptance of certain beliefs and codes rather than a practice of self-liberation. And here also the impact of the religious systems of the East has lent impetus to the birth of a more comprehensive awareness of our spiritual nature and its potential.

A major element in any time of profound transition is confusion. Faced with so many alternatives in belief and practice, the Tibetans brought into play their basic sense of perspective and inclination toward unity, just as we, with our characteristic drive to ascertain the unifying principles of things, always push toward an integrated, well-ordered view of the universe. Both cultures have succumbed at times to the same mistakes in assimilating this new material: oversimplification to the point of uselessness, mixing divergent elements instead of integrating them into a unified system, unproductive intellectual speculation, and dogmatic adherence to one interpretation over all others.

During such transitional periods persons of practical bent are primarily concerned with evaluating the various systems of thought to ascertain the "right practice." Milarepa appeared at such a time when a good number of practitioners were so engaged. Some pursued their quest in the large or small groups of monastic institutions, while others, like Milarepa, wandered the mountains and countryside in the lifestyle of the Indian *sannyasin—*

long haired, socially aloof, homeless and without possessions, begging in the streets of villages and meditating in isolated retreats. This is the most significant difference between Milarepa's cultural environment and ours. In the Tibet of Milarepa's day as in India before that, there was social acknowledgment and even respect for the pursuit of self-realization. Though it was beyond the scope of most people, a space existed outside the confines of social forms for those who were willing to give up home and possessions for the slim chance of gaining realization.

Even with social acceptability life wasn't easy for a yogi of Milarepa's time. There was competition from other hungry mendicants and from more established religious institutions. It wasn't always easy to beg a meal from poor peasants who were tired of tending the needs of wild-eyed strangers in their villages. For these villagers Milarepa was a constant wonder and challenge. He entertained them with song, scolded and criticized, cajoled, played sarcastic jokes, and encouraged them with his compassion. He taught them the straight Dharma, and through all of it shone the uniqueness of his personality, the penetrating intensity of his intellect, and the radiance of his realization.

Mila's life and his many exploits are best told in his autobiography and in the *Hundred Thousand Songs*. He frequently had to explain himself, and he told his life story many times, as in the first selection in this volume. He was born in 1052 in a small town in provincial Tibet. His family name Mila descended from a paternal ancestor who was credited with powers of exorcism, and he was given the surname Thöpa Ga, Joy-to-Hear. Because of his father's successful trading business, his family was wealthy by village standards; but his father's death, while Mila and his younger sister were still children, left them homeless. They were victimized by a paternal aunt and uncle, who forced the mother and her two children to work as servants and laborers.

Mila left and, on his mother's instruction, went to study with a shaman skilled in supernormal powers. Mila had a natural bent for mystical things and quickly acquired powers of a destructive nature, particularly that of causing devastating hailstorms. Thus equipped, Mila returned to his village to satisfy his mother's desire for vengeance. He committed the murder of his aunt's entire family and then fled. Eventually he regretted his actions and the enormous karmic obstruction they perpetrated. Realizing that this action had to be corrected in this same lifetime to prevent a very unfavorable rebirth, he sought religious instruction in Buddhism. His first teacher was of the old school, the Nyingma, who assured him that his system would give certain and immediate results. After a period of fruitless practice, the teacher told Mila that his karmic connection was stronger with another lama named Marpa Lotsawa, "The Translator of Mar," and sent Mila to find him.

Marpa was an unusual person. He was a married householder, a great tantric teacher, and the translator of many Sanskrit Buddhist works that have become a standard part of the Tibetan canon. He survived several difficult and dangerous trips to India on which many of his fellow Tibetans had died. In India his principal guru was Nāropa, and Nāropa's in turn was Tilopa, who had received his teachings from their originator, the transhistorical buddha Vajradhara, the primordial buddha of the Kagyu sect. Thus Marpa was the direct successor of the Kagyu lineage. Back in Tibet Marpa translated the works he had learned in India and transmitted their teachings to his disciples.

In teaching, he projected a stern and forbidding personality over his basically warm and compassionate nature. This method of working with his disciples proved especially appropriate for Milarepa, whose many negative elements and great karmic obstructions had to be purified. Marpa subjected Milarepa to several years of frustrating trials before he taught him directly. After such intense purification and appetite-whetting, Mila devoted himself wholly to the task of practicing these teachings newly transplanted from India onto Tibetan soil. He was successful, or so the Tibetans believe, and achieved his goal of full experiential verification of the Buddhist system of liberation, leaving in his wake generations of accomplished practitioners and a wealth of teaching in song.

Once Mila had left Marpa and was on his own, he pursued his practice continually, staying mostly in caves in the more desolate mountains of southwestern Tibet and western Nepal. His austere practice of wearing just a single cotton robe year round earned him the title "repa," which when added to his family name forms "Milarepa." Occasionally he would visit a village or encampment of herders to beg food, and in return would sing extemporaneous teaching songs, a custom already established in his day. Things were hard at times, but Mila always exhibited indomitable courage in facing the hardships of practice and adverse conditions. Eventually word of him spread among the people, and some believed him to be an accomplished siddha.

Fame didn't please him, however, and he wasn't easy to meet. One might think he was a yogi so concerned with his own welfare that he had lost all interest in human relationships and viewed social contact as unnecessary trouble. Mila did state such feelings in his songs, and it seems as if he were always rejecting would-be disciples and their offerings; but this is just one of the many paradoxes of his unique personality—paradoxes he used with great skill in training people. Mila had a wry sense of humor tending to sarcasm and was absolutely candid and direct in dealing with people. But he was not without method, differing on the surface from Marpa's but, judging from the number of his accomplished disciples, even more effective. He had a lot of followers for someone who made such an effort to avoid people. They were drawn to him, like satellites succumbing to the irresistible pull of a great planet: loners, scholars, disciples of other teachers. And there were even innumerable peasants and householders whose natural human drive for transcendence was kindled on meeting this great yogi.

In getting to know Milarepa, then, weigh his words against his actions; it is in their contradictions and complements that Milarepa's skillful handling of personality and relationships is brought to light.

The Buddhist System of Liberation

TO DEFINE PRECISELY a basic system of Buddhist practice is an impossibility because of the great number of schools and styles both in India and Tibet. However, it is possible to form a general picture of the Buddhist system of the Great Vehicle as explained by Milarepa in many of his songs and stories. Taking into account that his explanation and emphasis varied according to his audience, we can reconstruct a brief "stages of the path" text wherein the basic elements of the Smaller, Great, and Tantric Vehicles are placed into perspective in a consistent, effective system. This shows that even at this early stage in Tibet there was a tendency to integrate the three vehicles and diverse schools of Indian Buddhism into a unified system. The following excerpts are from "Mila's First Meditation" and "Rechungpa's Mahāmudrā Pride," both from the large collection *Stories and Songs from the Oral Tradition of Jetsün Milarepa*, from which all the material in this book is drawn.

The first step is to understand the leisure and opportunity for liberation provided by well-endowed human life:

> This fragile body of flesh and blood endowed with a subjective consciousness results from the twelvefold chain of dependent origination—ignorance and so on. It is the great ship of leisure and opportunity for those endowed with merit and the urge for liberation. However, for the evil-natured who use it to pile up sin upon sin it is a guide leading them to lower states. It stands on the boundary between development and degeneration. I have understood in the nick of time this critical situation, which can lead to lasting good or lasting ill.

Mila explains the general condition of samsara, or cyclic, mundane existence, in this way:

> Living beings of the six realms (the life-forms of samsaric existence), afflicted with ignorance and attached to illusory appearances, have been bewildered throughout beginningless samsara. They take what

is selfless to be a self—what is egoless to be an ego—and thus are adrift on the ocean of samsaric misery through compulsive attachment to the imprints of evil action.

Every action, every experience, has left its traces imprinted on our minds in the form of "seeds" for the recurrence of such experiences. The primary imprinting is that of ignorance, which engenders the mistaken world view of the existence of egos in persons and identities in things just as they appear to the ordinary individual. In the wake of this mistaken gut feeling about the nature of our experience the afflictive emotions of attraction, aversion, and so on are brought into play.

Now to explain the inner workings of this: beings wander in samsara due to the action of the twelve causal links of dependent origination. First, ignorance—that is, "not knowing," "not understanding," "not realizing" (the actual condition of the objects and events of our experience)—provides the condition for the synthetic operation (of the elements of samsaric existence). This process continues up to the inevitable miseries of recurrent birth, sickness, aging, and death.

This chain of dependent origination is the process by which beings are born repeatedly into the samsaric condition with its six life-states: hell beings, hungry ghosts, animals, humans, gods, and anti-gods. The state and condition of their births and lives is determined by their re-actions (*karma*) to experiences in previous lives.

The majority of beings take lower rebirth (as hell beings, hungry ghosts, or animals) through the force of bad action. Such lower states are miserable, and even lives in the (three) higher states have a nature of misery.

The way to correct this sequence is to understand at the beginning the difficulty of obtaining the leisure and opportunity (of well-endowed human life)—that such leisure and opportunity found only once in a hundred births is impermanent and that the time of death is uncertain. You must reflect on the fact that there's no telling where you'll be reborn after dying, and since we are inexorably impelled by the force of action, you must consider the cause-effect relationship of action.

So according to Mila, the first step is to have a thorough understanding of the samsaric condition and its causes, to meditate on misery, death, and impermanence to quicken the initial impulse for freedom into a powerful drive for liberation, and to understand that our present human existence is the best possible opportunity for overthrowing the oppression of ignorance and achieving such liberation.

Motivated by these understandings one then enters the door of actual Buddhist practice:

> For protection from lower births
> Caused by the force of evil deeds,
> Lama and the Triple Gem are the sole refuge.

In all Buddhist schools the beginner takes refuge in the Triple Gem consisting of the Buddha, who is able to guide others through his own freedom from samsara (*saṁsāra*), the Dharma (his teachings), and the Sangha (the community of practitioners). This refuge doesn't involve a denial of worldly pursuits but places them in perspective with regard to these effective guides to liberation. Since the Triple Gem cannot at first be a living presence to us, the lama (*guru*) is their living representative. Thus in Tibet the lama is placed first in importance even to the buddhas, for it is through him that we'll eventually meet the buddhas. Mila calls this understanding of commitment to a lama "the first key of great importance."

> After this it's necessary to rely on a basis constituted by whichever of the vows for personal liberation are appropriate (to oneself), with an urge for liberation from samsara compelled by reflection on death, impermanence, the cause-effect relationship of action, and the difficulty of finding the leisure and opportunity (of human life again).

The commitment to personal liberation (*prātimokśa*) refers to the vows of the Small Vehicle, which serve as guidelines for behavior conducive to (*nirvāṇa*), one's own liberation from misery. Hence the name "Small Vehicle"—one that can carry just oneself. It's necessary to expand this motivation further. The Great Vehicle encompasses all sentient beings in its scope, for in fact, all life is inextricably bound together, and the struggle for enlightenment must be pursued for the sake of everyone. Mila explains this as follows:

I understand that such orientation toward one's own peace and happiness constitutes the Small Vehicle, and that the Great Vehicle involves dedication of all one's activities for the welfare of others with the love and compassion of the mind aimed at enlightenment by the desire to liberate all beings from samsara.

This emphasis on the mind aimed at enlightenment (*bodhicitta*) distinguishes the Great Vehicle from the Small Vehicle. It is the sine qua non of Great Vehicle practice, for the penetrating wisdom by which we will eventually see the true void condition of all things must be balanced by the love and compassion of the mind-for-enlightenment in order to yield the perfect, nonexclusive freedom from samsara known as enlightenment. Even in the Tantric Vehicle, which is a refinement in method but basically the same in philosophy as the Great Vehicle, the mind-for-enlightenment is a necessary prerequisite for practice. The Sanskrit term for this, *bodhicitta*, can be defined as the condition of mind wherein all actions are performed spontaneously for the benefit of all. It is almost an instinctive drive for one's own freedom so that one may have the ability to guide others. On the other hand, bodhicitta is not itself directly productive of liberation, for unless tempered by wisdom it will only bind the practitioner more tightly to samsara.

Persons traveling a path involving generation of this mind-for-enlightenment through tantric or nontantric methods are called *bodhisattvas*, or "enlightenment warriors." (Sanskrit *sattva* means "living being," but has the secondary meaning of heroic or courageous, and is rendered thus in the Tibetan.) Mila sums it up in this way:

Having conceived of samsara as a prison, understand that all beings lost in it are none other than our own parents who have given us birth throughout beginningless time. With love and compassion for those lost in samsara, generate the mind aimed at supreme enlightenment for the sake of their liberation.

Then ride the great waves of practices aimed at enlightenment: the three basic path-practices, the four social means, and the six transcendences, thus compiling the two stores and purifying the two obscurations.

This passage summarizes the main practices of the Great Vehicle. The three basic practices comprise morality as behavioral practice, and concentration and wisdom as mental practices. The four social means—giving, relevant communication, assisting the development of others, and serving as an example for their inspiration—are practices oriented primarily toward the welfare of others. The six transcendences—giving, moral behavior, patience, effort, concentration, and wisdom—are practiced primarily for one's own development, although of course in the Great Vehicle there is no exclusive self-interest.

These practices have a double effect. First, they increase the two stores of personal power—the store of merit based on ethical behavior and proper performance of ritual, and the store of gnosis based on examination of the samsaric condition and its correction, from the first intellectual gleanings up to transcendent, supramundane wisdom beyond the range of words and thoughts. Secondly, they reduce the two obscurations—the obscuration of afflictive mental states, which blocks realization of nirvana, and the objective obscuration, which masks the reality of things, thus blocking the omniscience of perfect buddhahood.

Mila explains how the six transcendences, particularly those of concentration and wisdom, must be coordinated in a systematic practice of the path:

> Giving, moral behavior, and patience are the means of compiling the store of merit. Concentration and wisdom are the means of compiling the store of gnosis. Effort furthers all of them. The highest gnosis is the very mind of buddha. Those wishing to obtain it should apply themselves to these various methods.

Special attention is given to the development of concentration and wisdom. Basic meditation may be divided into that of focusing, or quieting the mind, through one-pointed concentration and the analytic process of generating wisdom through transcendent insight. This quieting, known in Sanskrit as *samatha,* is so called because by one-pointed concentration the activity of the mind is stilled. As certain mental functions are altered, the mind assumes different, meta-stable modes of operation. These eight "different modes" are termed absorption levels (*dhyāna*) and are similar in both Buddhist and Hindu mental cosmology. They are entirely samsaric, though of a much more refined nature than ordinary consciousness, and are the range of the traditional yogi's meditation. By practicing these states, all yogis receive their powers and bliss.

Because of the mental pleasure and supernormal powers they confer, the absorption levels can be construed as a path to liberation, which they are not. They are rather the solid bases from which the transcendent mental leap to direct confrontation of voidness through wisdom can occur. Since they are more developed and tranquil than ordinary mental operation, they are like the glass chimney of an oil lamp, steadying the tiny flame of wisdom against the winds of afflictive mental functionings.

Wisdom is developed by the practice of insight, a process of examination and analysis of our perceptions, a pressing of the intellect to the limits of its range until the flash of direct experience of reality occurs. This is the experience of the egolessness of persons and the voidness, or lack of identities, in things. It is the only meditational state capable of clearing the traces of experience that give rise to afflictive mental states and illusions about reality. Thus the practice of insight exceeds the practice of quieting, which can merely suppress the active forms of afflictive mental states.

The yogi must travel five paths to enlightenment. The process of compiling the two stores of merit and gnosis is the accumulation path, and the meditational application of these two stores to direct perception of voidness is the application path. The direct perception of voidness itself is the path of seeing, and the development and repeated application of such direct perception to clear the compulsive action of the imprintings of experience is termed the "meditation path." The final elimination of all traces of the two obscurations is the final path, or path beyond practice, equivalent to buddhahood. Mila sums it up:

> In brief, the basis is faith, the assistor is effort, the antidote is the acquisition (of virtue) and expiation (of sin), the direct cause is the integration of wisdom with method (the active aspect of the mind-for-enlightenment), and the subsidiary cause is the practice of the accumulation and application paths. When the path of seeing is thereby attained, that is the direct experience of the wisdom of insight.

With attainment of the path of seeing, the bodhisattva-warrior stands on the first of ten bodhisattva stages, and after traversing them one by one attains the eleventh stage, the stage of enlightenment.

The Kagyu Lineage of Buddhist Practice

MILAREPA'S SYSTEM OF PRACTICE, known as the Kagyu or "Lineage of the Word," was given by the transhistorical figure Vajradhara to the guru Tilopa, who in turn taught Nāropa. Marpa, Milarepa's lama, received these teachings from Nāropa, translated their scriptures, and established them in Tibet. Milarepa himself had two principal successors and many other accomplished disciples who continued the Kagyu tradition in a number of variant lineages. Later lamas imparted their own personal styles, so that the Kagyu practices of the present day cannot be viewed as identical to Mila's own style. However, they have remained largely similar. We'll attempt to form a picture of Milarepa's system from his explanations in the *Stories and Songs from the Oral Tradition of the Great Yogi Milarepa*.

The Tantric Vehicle

The practices are essentially tantric. The Tantric Vehicle is the same in philosophy as the Great Vehicle but differs vastly in the actual techniques of practice. Because it is equivalent to the Great Vehicle in aim but more effective in practice, Mila said, "To leave the inferior path (of the Small Vehicle) and (really) enter the Great Vehicle, one must enter the path of the Peerless Vajra Vehicle (*anuttaratantra*)."[1]

All elements of the Great Vehicle path are present in the Tantric Vehicle. The five paths and ten bodhisattva stages are condensed into two phases: production and completion. During the extensive production phase the yogi first purifies himself with guru yoga and generates the mind aimed at enlightenment. Then the currents, channels, and centers (*prāṇa, nāḍī, cakra*) of the tantric psycho-physiological system are developed and mastery over their functions sought through the physical and mental exercises of the path of method. The deities of the Tantric Vehicle's extensive pantheon, the male and female personifications of psychic processes as *herukas* and *ḍākinīs*, are "produced" by the yogi through the practice of controlled visualization until their reality overshadows that of the superficial apparent world. This production leads the yogi to confront the processes embodied in each deity and to transform his own environment into the divine realm of that deity. In particular, the yogi forms a relationship with one specific deity, known as his "personal deity" (Skt. *iṣṭadevatā*; Tib. *yidam*), through practices and visualizations associated with that deity. When the yogi is able to visualize his personal deity to the point where the visualization seems to have a life of its own, and when he is able to see his environment as divine, he then practices the "divine pride" of direct identification of his own body and mind with those of his personal deity.

When the reality of the apparent world has been overshadowed by the intensity of his visualization, the yogi then enters the completion phase where the illusory nature, or voidness, of his visualization can be realized, and with it the voidness of the ordinary, apparent world. This is due to the fact that the apparent world is by nature an illusory "visualization" derived from compulsive attachment to ingrained preconceptions about the nature of things.

Realization of voidness is not the only result in the completion phase, for owing to the previous production phase, the yogi is endowed with powers and method as well. In particular, at the culmination of the completion phase he has developed the three bodies, or modes of existence, of a buddha. The dharma-body (*dharmakāya*) is the embodiment of his realization that all appearances—thoughts and phenomena—are inherently devoid of any independent identity. The enjoyment-body (*saṁbhogakāya*) is the means by which he communicates with advanced practitioners in their meditation. The emanation-body (*nirmāṇakāya*) appears in the world as though it were an ordinary physical body; but actually this physical body is not compelled by the force of past action and afflictive mental states but rather by the force of will and previous supplication for the welfare of beings (*prāṇidhāna*). The latter two together are termed the form-body, and the unity of all three the essential-body.

Guru and Empowerment

In tantric practice the relationship with an experienced and qualified guru (Tib. *lama*) is of special importance. It is he who guides us to the correct path and serves as the pivotal point in opening our minds to the reality of ourselves and our world.

> The holy lama is the embodiment of all buddhas.
> His voice expresses the inexpressible.
> His mind is the directionless sunlight of method and wisdom.
>
> One who realizes that all actions
> Of a (true) lama's body, speech, and mind—

Farming, stealing, even killing—are virtuous,
Who sees them in particular as a buddha's acts,
Is the best disciple for practicing the profound path.

But not every lama is a true teacher and not every student a worthy vessel of Dharma. The statement above applies only to advanced tantric students in a long-standing relationship with a guru. Even a qualified lama and a good student might find their relationship unproductive due to elements in their personal makeup. The relationship must provide the situations for the initial analysis of the student's actions and motivations and be capable of inducing the subtle, penetrating revelations in the course of development.

The lama must also be able to perform the rites of empowerment effectively in order to open the disciple to successful tantric practice. As Milarepa explains, "empowerment" means "conferral of ability." Empowerment only gives the initiate a glimpse of the import of the practice; he must still cultivate skill in its performance and actual realization. The course of Mila's initiation by the four tantric empowerments, and his motivation, are recounted in the second of the "Six Secret Songs":

I'm now Milarepa, but I'm certain
This body of leisure and opportunity will be spent.
This canyon of samsara is a vast abyss
And I fear the narrow track of birth and death.

When I think that this wandering in samsara
Lasts till the forces of action and effect are stilled,
I know it's time to end this illusion of ego.

And how could I bear the way these beings
Of the six realms, our kind mothers, are tormented by misery?
Thus I sought the path for quickly achieving
This body of conquerors, leaders of beings.

First, by conferral of the vase empowerment,
My ordinary body was identified with deity's.
Then by the secret empowerment of the stream of speech,
Currents flowing in the right and left channels were drawn to
    the central.

By igniting the bliss of the third empowerment (of wisdom),
I saw the naked maiden of the egoless sphere,
And by recognition of the four bodies symbolically expressed
In the fourth empowerment (of words), I faced the unity of the
    three bodies.[2]

After entering the initiatory doors, I practiced the two phases
And unified with space and awareness
The deity's body produced earlier on the path.

This unification with space and awareness is Vajradhara.
For this purpose the emanation-body of Shakyamuni
    (*Śākyamuni*) appeared.

This is victory over birth, death, and bardo.
Having obtained the three bodies for myself,
I've no hope or fear about other results.

Following empowerment, when the yogi begins practice in earnest, he must observe the major and minor vows of the Tantric Vehicle as well as those involved in his particular practice. Mila gives some idea of these commitments in the third of the "Six Secret Songs":

Through the method and wisdom of my unique lama
My vision toward friends and others was purified.
All these beings are my mothers—
Blind of eye, crazed by afflictions—
Yogi, how can you bear it? Dedicate yourself in service to beings.

Woman is essentially wisdom,
Source of spontaneous gnosis and illusory-body.[3]
Never consider her inferior;
Strive especially to see her as Vajra Varāhī.[4]

Never worship a deity with ordinary food and clothes,
As common men worship a king.
When power objects are used in ordinary ways,
It's like pouring clean milk into a dirty vessel.

(You must) keep and never be without
Bone ornaments, vajra-bell, and so on.

The disciple is also committed to secrecy concerning the nature of his empowerments, personal deity, and tantric practice. Although the tantras are "self-secret," that is, their real import cannot be gleaned from their scriptures by a noninitiate, they can be harmful to practice and mental stability if misapplied.

The Course of Practice: Quiescence and Insight

After initial refuge-taking, disciples who are vessels (of dharma) under the guidance of a qualified lama should generate the mind aimed at enlightenment, compile the stores (of merit and gnosis) by performing the seven acts of worship, of guru yoga, mandala offerings, prayer, and so on, and clear away the blockage (of previous bad action) by meditation and repetition of the hundred-syllable Vajrasattva mantra.

It is of utmost importance to persevere in all this for months and even years until the signs of development occur. Even after such signs and indications have occurred, you must still achieve spontaneous concentration by the gradual process of actual realization states based on the store of previously compiled merit.

The achievement of "spontaneous" or "effortless" concentration is not a spontaneous or effortless matter. The process of quiescence through one-pointed concentration, the prerequisite for the analytic practice aimed at transcendent insight, is a major, consuming task. Mila explains it as follows:

(In the practice of quiescence) beginners achieve mental stability by degrees, their stream of thought (at first) breaking through like a mountain cascade, until eventually the mind remains naturally focused wherever it is placed. This is termed "mental stability," and since it is the foundation of the absorption levels (*dhyāna*), there is no advancement without it.

The process advances through seven phases before reaching the level of spontaneous concentration. Advancement involves learning to correct various degrees of antithetical mental functionings—particularly "mental sinking" or sluggishness through the mind's tendency to be overly absorbed in its object, and "excitation" through an over-reactivity or scattering of the attention from the object to other things. It also involves the suppression of mental discursiveness or thought-flow instigated by the habitual, compulsive tendency to identify and name the objects of experience. To achieve correct concentration, the yogi must develop the antidotes: recollective awareness, which serves to hold attention to the object by "remembering" the situation and instructions for concentration, and critical awareness, which assesses the mental situation at any moment and determines how it might be going astray.

Quiescence involves suppression of thought-flow by concentration, while the complementary process, analytic insight, involves penetration of the thought process through the exercise of intellect while in a state of concentrative quiescence. The practice of insight is aimed at the experience of transcendent wisdom through investigation of the true condition of persons and things—their egolessness or voidness. It begins with learning the facts and teachings and then reflecting on their import in detail and depth. Study was not rejected by Milarepa, only over-interest in books. Real training of the intellect is essential to the process of analytic insight. Mila explains this as follows:

> Analytic meditation that subjects to repeated examination the mistaken assumptions involved in learning and reflecting (on the teachings of) an experienced, skillful lama concerning the explicit import of the (scriptures), when firmly combined with previously developed quiescence concentration, is termed focusing meditation. During such experience the understanding of the actual condition (of things, i.e., their voidness of identity), the explicit goal of such analysis, is termed understanding. The various mental events and apparitional experiences occurring in the mind equipoised in such correct understanding and firmly based on quiescence are termed (developmental) experiences. The direct confrontation of the goal, the natural state, supported by these experiences is realization.

The Experience of Transcendence

Realization, then, is the direct experience of the goal of analysis, termed the natural state in the Kagyu system. It is the transcendent, inexpressible experience of direct perception of the voidness, or lack of an inherent independent ego, of persons and identity in things. All direct experiences of voidness have three phases: 1) a preparatory process wherein the elements of concentration and analysis are applied in combination to produce the tolerance, or mental readiness, for the experience; 2) the actual transcendent realization state wherein all ordinary perceptions and concepts of the apparent world are suppressed by perception of their voidness; and 3) the post-attainment state wherein the "reverberation" of this experience continues into the world of appearances, loosening the hold of the conceptual process within the realm of superficial experience. The transcendent experience itself is at first an instantaneous flash which is gradually extended in practice as the yogi's mind becomes more experienced and agile. The post-attainment state is of great importance and must be developed until the experience of voidness is extended and unified with perception of the apparent world, an accomplishment equivalent to the attainment of buddhahood.

The Tantric Approach

All this accords with practice as defined in the Great Vehicle, but in Milarepa's Kagyu system it is approached tantrically:

> To realize the pure view (of voidness) one needs the correct, complete rites of the series of four empowerments performed by a qualified lama which confer the wisdom and method to recognize it. "Empowerment" means "conferral of the ability" to attain the profound view; one must then cultivate it gradually. When thus empowered to investigate personal egolessness, an (independently existing) personal ego is sought through the many examples of scripture and reasonings of logic. It cannot be thus identified, yielding the understanding of personal egolessness. The mind must then be placed in a state of balanced concentration on this unfindability of a personal ego, and while in this state freedom from thought-constructs occurs spontaneously through stoppage of preconceptions (about the nature and identities of things).
>
> When this state lasts for days, months, and even years without awareness (of the passage of time), so that one must even be brought out of it by others, that is the inception of quiescence. When this state is tempered by recollective awareness and critical awareness so that it is unaffected by mental sinking/sluggishness, such illumination, self-naturelessness, clear freedom from thought-constructs, and naked, brilliant purity is the (developed) experience

of quiescence. This is sometimes construed as analytic insight, but since real insight cannot occur in an ordinary individual (who has not experienced voidness directly), I feel that true insight is encountered only on the first bodhisattva stage when the path of seeing is attained. I feel that other experiences in quiescence practice—visions of deities, etc.—are merely signs of meditation and meaningless in themselves.

Moreover, I've realized that prior to any experience of quiescence one must be motivated by love and compassion and directed by the mind-for-enlightenment aimed at others' welfare in any activity. During such practice one should practice without fixed objective through pure view. And afterwards the practice should be stamped with the seal of supplication (*prāṇidhāna*) by dedicating (all results) to the welfare of others.

I've realized that just as mere knowledge of food doesn't help a hungry man, it's not enough to understand the goal of voidness (intellectually); one must cultivate (its direct experience repeatedly). Also, the cultivation of analytic insight requires unstinting effort in compiling virtue and eliminating faults (while performing action) in the post-attainment state.

In short, I now understand that the inexpressible, inconceivable voidness equanimities cultivated in yoga constitute the view of the (Tantric) Vehicle related to the four empowerments.

Mahāmudrā Practice of the Kagyupas

After the yogi has trained himself in the essentials of quiescence and is able to attain at least the first absorption level, and after he has acquainted himself to some extent with the analysis aimed at direct perception of voidness, he is directed to the central practice of the Kagyu tradition, the mahāmudrā ("great gesture" or "great seal"). Like the Great Liberation teachings of the Nyingma, or Old School, and the exercises in analysis of the Kadam and Gelug sects, mahāmudrā practice is aimed directly at revelation of the natural reality of the apparent world. The system is aligned with the Peerless (*anuttara*) Yoga Tantras, and its practice and scriptures date back to the eighty-four siddhas of India. It is an example of the deepest, most penetrating phase of yoga, and its expression in words is characteristically paradoxical and metaphorical. The key instructions are given orally from teacher to student, and the fourth empowerment, the empowerment of words, relates directly to it:

By conferral of the fourth and supreme empowerment,
One becomes focused in the fabrication-free state
Through perception of the import of mahāmudrā.

It is not as "sudden" a practice as its scriptures seem to imply. The struggle to attain its goal, the natural state (Tib. *gnas lugs*), wherein the perception of voidness is totally unified with perception of the apparent world, is long and arduous:

Without confronting the goal, the natural state,
You won't find escape to freedom
From the highs and lows of samsara.

If you wish to see the goal of reality,
Cleanse previous obstructive sins with the
    hundred-syllable mantra
And compile the two stores by mandala, and so on.

Then after aligning your mind with lama's
Through intense, longing prayer,
Practice the graded instructions for quiescence
From mere inception of stability
Onward in gradual stages.

Because the natural state is the root,
It looks so easy but is very hard.
But when awareness is focused on reality
After analysis by learning and reflecting,
This is the one realization that liberates totally;
It looks so hard but is very easy.

Upon such good stabilization
Collect the nectar of explicit scriptures.
Then through examination by learning and reflecting
On the profound meaning personally taught
By a realized, experienced lama,
Take up practice as long as life lasts
Through combination of analytic and focusing meditations.

Integrate compassion and voidness,
And with mind aimed at enlightenment for the sake of beings
And gnosis without fixed objective,
Mount the horse of good supplication.
By the forces of thorough comprehension,
Knowledge of the keys to meditation,
And constant cultivation like a river stream
Of that gradual path process,
You'll complete the developmental signs of the path.

Realizations will then gradually occur,
Conventional appearances seen as dream illusions,
Dependent origination known to be the inner workings
    of samsara,
And illusory appearances seen as baseless, rootless.

You'll know that beings are inseparable from buddhas,
That not even the names "samsara" and "nirvana" exist.

This comprehension of the natural condition—
The actual state—is understanding.
The various events in one-pointed concentration
Are meditational experiences;
When they lead to confrontation of the goal,
That's realization.

In a rather unusual text-like precept from *Recognizing Mahāmudrā's Illuminating Wisdom*, Milarepa explains that "mahāmudrā" means three things: the ultimate reality of things, termed the basis; the practice leading to its realization, termed the path; and the illumined state of mind, the result.

First, mahāmudrā as the *basis* means the natural state that is the basic condition of things, the intention of Buddha, the real nature of beings. It is without color or form, without circumference or center, free from partiality, not experienced as existing or not existing, not illusory, not liberated, not produced by a cause, and not influenced by conditions. Wise buddhas cannot improve it, nor stupid beings impair it. It is not improved by realization, nor impaired by illusion. Because that is the basic condition (of things), the basis is mahāmudrā .

Second, mahāmudrā as *path* means the possibility of practice on the strength of that basis. When focusing, focus without objective. When stabilizing, be stabilized without distraction. When shifting, shift without grasping. When manifestations occur, experience them as reality. When a liberation occurs, allow it to occur naturally.

Third, mahāmudrā as *result* means the freedom from anything that is liberated and any agent of liberation, from hope and from fear. It is beyond intellection, beyond facts, free from (the perception of) identities, and transcends compulsive conceptualization. Thus it is beyond thought and expression.

These three—basis, path, and result—are indivisible in practice.

Gampopa, Milarepa's direct successor, explains the natural state and the practice leading to it in more detail in his *Defining the Mahāmudrā Path*:

There are five points in identifying the actual state. In mahāmudrā there is no cause, but faith and aspiration are causes of mahāmudrā. In mahāmudrā there are no conditions, but the holy lama is the condition for mahāmudrā. In mahāmudrā there is no method, but the unmodified mind is the method of mahāmudrā. In mahāmudrā there is no path, but the undistracted mind is the path of mahāmudrā. In mahāmudrā there is no result, but the self-liberation of mind into reality is the result of mahāmudrā.

There are four points concerning the process of practice leading to reality:

1. The preparatory practice is to meditate guru yoga three times each day and each night with faith, admiration, and determination.
2. The actual meditative state is the precise focusing and holding of the mind undistractedly in the unmodified state.
3. Afterwards, exercise the agility of mind, realizing that whatever appears is one's own mind.
4. Persevere with meditation according to the way in which experiences occur until conceptualization is exhausted.

Concerning the ways in which experiences occur, there are both negative and positive experiences. The former are any negative experiences that occur, like mental sinking and excitement, illness, anxiety and panic, confusion, and so on.[5] Understand that they are all products of meditation and thus just experiences. Through meditation utilizing the stepping stone of development of the correct view of reality, they will subsequently become positive experiences.

Positive experiences consist of the experience of initial mental stabilization, the experience of void nature based on that, the experience of direct realization based on that, and the experience of correcting insistence (on preconceptions) based on that. Just correction of insistence isn't enough; it's necessary to meditate until buddhahood is attained at the end of conceptualization and facts through the self-liberation of mind into reality.

Nāropa, Marpa's guru, was poetic and closer to the siddhas' style of expressing mahāmudrā in his *Epitome of Mahāmudrā*:

1. The mahāmudrā view:

> I will speak of mahāmudrā:
> All things are one's own mind.
> Perceptions of external objects are mistaken concepts,
> Like dream, devoid of substance.
>
> Mind itself is the action of associative memory
> Lacking self-nature, powered by currents (*prāṇa*),
> Devoid of identity like the sky.
> All things are equivalent like space.
>
> That which is called mahāmudrā
> Does not exist by some inherent nature,
> Thus the reality of mind itself
> Is the nature of mahāmudrā.

2. Mahāmudrā meditation:

> In it there's no modification or change.
> When someone experiences the sight of reality,
> The whole apparent world is mahāmudrā,
> The great all-pervading dharma-body.
>
> Remain relaxed in natural unmodification.
> Abide in meditation without seeking

The inconceivable dharma-body;
Meditation that seeks is a mistaken concept.

Just like the sky and visions therein
Meditation and nonmeditation are not two—
Of what is it free or not free?
That's how a yogi seeks realization.

3. Mahāmudrā behavior:

All actions virtuous and evil
Are liberated by knowing mahāmudrā;
Afflictive states are great gnosis
Supporting the yogi as a forest supports a fire.

Where are going and staying?
Why go into retreat to meditate?
One who hasn't realized reality
Won't be liberated more than temporarily.

At death one who's realized reality
Remains unwavered in that state;
No meditation, no correction by antidote,
No "equanimity" or "nonequanimity."

4. Mahāmudrā as result:

Here nothing at all truly exists:
Appearances are the naturally liberated dharma-realm,
Thoughts the great naturally liberated gnosis—
The nondual, all equivalent dharma-body.

Like the current of a mighty river
Whatever you do is purposeful.
This is eternal buddhahood,
Great bliss beyond samsara's reach.

Things are naturally devoid of identity,
The concept of voidness itself naturally pure—
Free of concepts, no mental fixation at all—
This is the path of all buddhas.

Subsidiary Practices

The Kagyu lineage also has a number of yogic practices to prepare for and accompany the practice of mahāmudrā, such as the famous six yogas of Nāropa. This type of yoga belongs to the path of method and is concerned with gaining mastery of the psycho-physical currents (*prāṇa*), loosening the "knots" of the channels (*nāḍī*) through which they flow, and directing them to certain channels and centers (*cakra*).

The first, *tummo* or heat yoga, is frequently mentioned by Milarepa. Its practitioners, known as "repas," wear just a thin cotton robe even in winter. Mila explains briefly to Rechungpa in the fifth of the "Six Secret Songs":

> This method of practice is a secret shortcut.
> In particular, the eye which sees Vajra Varāhī[6]
> Will later see three tummo stages—low, middle, and high—
> Tongue of flame, full bliss, and so on
> As though from inside the sun.
>
> Knots of the right and left channels are loosened to their
>   natural state
> By Vajrasattva mantra,[7] which draws current in and out of the
>   central channel.
> Don't rely on any mental support
> Other than Vajrasattva mantra repetition.
>
> Binding the flow of life-force from the heart (center)
> To the central channel by the yoga of coarse and fine currents,
> Experience like a cloudless sky develops.
> Equalize the fluctuation of red and white elements[8] in the navel
>   (center);
> Realization and bliss-warmth experience then dawns in the mind.

This passage, employing technical yogic terminology, indicates how the mind and currents are interdependent in a relationship termed "mind-current complex." Any realization necessarily involves an alteration of the currents, and it is the purpose of these yogas to develop control of them. In addition, the resultant blissful state that comes with generation of tummo heat is in itself valuable in development.

The second yoga of Nāropa, the illusory-body yoga, deals directly with the misperception of the self and environment by understanding ordinary conceptual perception of the body through its similarity to hallucination, as Mila explains in the last of the "Six Secret Songs":

> There are in general three types of illusion:
> The confused illusion concerning appearances and voidness,
> (Visualized) illusions of mind-created deities,
> And hallucinatory illusions from (disturbance of) mind and
>   currents.
> To understand the workings of these three,
> You must stop the flow in right and left channels.
> Stopping in and out breath would be better.
> Mind and currents are then absorbed in the clear-light state.

The third, dream yoga, involves the similarity of the dream process to the mistaken preconceptual experience of the self and its environment in ordinary consciousness:

> When the imprintings of illusory dreams are activated,
> You must realize the nature of appearances and voidness
> Through recognition of illusion of dream in the birthless
>   void state
> And create (your own dream) emanations of void appearances.
>
> You must practice the precepts for the three transformations:
> The general transformation of the apparent world into the
>   divine,
> The particular (manifestation) of the deity's body in dream
>   through mind and currents,
> And emanated bodies, clairvoyance, and so on.

The three remaining yogas of this group—the clear-light, transference (of consciousness), and bardo (after-death state) yogas—likewise treat the experiences of our lives, yogic and nonyogic, as opportunities to gain mastery of mind and currents and to assist the endeavor to realize the end of illusion.

Milarepa's Personal Style

AS MENTIONED BEFORE, and as the stories will show, Milarepa was an unusual, almost eccentric, personality. His revelations of the nature of illusion and reality and of the keys to effective practice were always penetrating and to the point. The stories attest to the severity of the hardships he endured and the extreme to which he pushed himself in practice. This excerpt from the "Six Secret Songs" is a good example. It's a version of Milarepa's "ultimate precept," this time given to Rechungpa:

> While staying in the miracle cave (of Ti Se mountain) Jetsün Milarepa said to Rechungpa, "You've obtained the precepts of the Ḍākiṇīs' Ear-Whispered Tantras to complete the transmission of my instructional lineage. Now you must practice them to achieve results in this lifetime."
>
> Rechungpa asked him, "Please sing me a song expressing the key for obtaining the supreme siddhi (enlightenment) in this lifetime."
>
> Jetsün replied, "My ultimate precept is this," and he turned around, exposing his buttocks, which were prominently covered with lumps of hard callus from long periods of sitting meditation. Seeing this, Rechungpa was overwhelmed with immense admiration and respect for the austerities in practice endured by his lama. Tears welled up in his eyes and he thought with conviction, "I, too, must practice like this."

The Songs

Milarepa purifies himself by building houses for Marpa

About the Songs

THE COMPLETE TEXT from which these selections were taken, *Stories and Songs from the Oral Tradition of Jetsün Milarepa,* opens with this foreword:

> Here (in Tibet) the great, famous siddha known as Milarepa, Lord of Yogis, carried on the cargo of the vehicles. Maintaining humility, he practiced austerities and was as accustomed to living in caves as a man is to wearing a hat. He perfected the practice of one-pointed concentration and poured forth twenty-eight hundred songs born of his experience and realization in eighteen, twenty-one, or forty major song cycles. Two thousand of these are said to be preserved by the ḍākinīs and are unknown in the human world. The other eight hundred are related by yogis even to this day, and utilized by them in their practice.

These eight hundred songs are preserved in writing in three main works. Milarepa's autobiography as told to his closest disciple Rechungpa was first translated into English by Kazi Dawa Samdup under the title *Tibet's Great Yogi Milarepa* (Evans-Wentz, ed., Oxford) and has been retranslated by Lobsang Lhalungpa as *The Life of Milarepa* (Dutton, NY, 1977). The larger collection of stories and songs, the *Hundred Thousand Songs,* was translated by Garma C.C. Chang and published in various editions. These two works contain the Milarepa material familiar in both the East and the West. In addition, there is a rare, little known collection "from the oral tradition" containing, with a few exceptions, completely different material. This is the *Stories and Songs from the Oral Tradition of Jetsün Milarepa,*[9] from which the material of this book, and its companion volume, *Miraculous Journey* (Lotsawa, 1986), was taken. In addition, several of Milarepa's practice manuals are contained in the *Treasury of Precepts,* and various groupings of stories and songs are in lesser known Tibetan editions.

In attempting to piece together a picture of Milarepa's personality, his singing, and his teaching style, this present work is valuable, perhaps more so than the two standard works. The *Hundred Thousand Songs,* and possibly the autobiography also, were transcribed from the orally repeated versions at an early date by the "Mad Yogi of Tsang," Tsang Nyön Heruka Rüs Pai rGyän. That he incorporated a good deal of his own literary skills into the transcription may be deduced from stylistic comparison of the few parallel passages in the *Stories and Songs*. For example, "Mila's Meeting with Phadampa Sangye" in this book corresponds to chapter 53 of Chang's edition of the *Hundred Thousand Songs*. These two versions of the same incident show marked differences. The version in this volume is about half as long as the standard version in the *Hundred Thousand Songs* in both narrative and song. More significantly, its poetic style is less elaborate and makes less use of developed and embellished poetic elements. Its tone is more spontaneous and its impact more direct, especially when read aloud. In such comparison it gives the impression of being extemporaneous, rather than composed.

The material in *Stories and Songs* existed in an oral state longer than that of the two standard works; thus it might, and does seem to, contain a certain amount of interpolated material added in the repeated tellings by yogis. Passages of this sort can be distinguished from the bulk of the text by their inferior poetry, their unusually lengthy treatment of the topic, and their uninspired, poorly paced delivery. Almost without exception the additions consist of admonitions concerning the effects of bad action, rebirth in the lower states of existence, the miseries of samsaric life, and other basic topics especially suitable for inexperienced lay audiences. Their fire-and-brimstone tone reminds us that these songs were recited by the yogis who preserved them in memory most frequently in return for offerings of food from peasants and herdsmen of the Tibetan and Nepali countryside.

In transcribing the material contained in *Stories and Songs*, the unnamed compiler in the large monastic center of Trashi Gyi in Amdo, Tibet made no attempt to impose a polished literary style. Some songs or stories are just sketchy fragments; others, however, are exceptional pieces and may have been omitted from the *Hundred Thousand Songs* because they did not deal with a famous incident or a first meeting with a major disciple, or perhaps because they were unknown to the earlier compiler. That they are authentic may be judged from their quality and style, with the understanding that, in the oral tradition that continues to this day, there are many variant versions of the same songs.

Another significant characteristic of the material in *Stories and Songs* is that it makes less attempt than the *Hundred Thousand Songs* to idolize Mila's personality and behavior, or to make them more consistently palatable to the reader. Here his actions are more abrupt, less polite, his humor and wisdom more devastatingly cutting, and his reactions more paradoxical. The inconsistencies and contradictions are here—there is a real, human person just behind the lines. There are new attitudes also, perhaps because they were not altered by a transcriber's sentiments, indicating, for example, that Mila was not as uneducated as most believe and that he did teach the importance of study before intensive meditation practice.

Good teachings always vary in subject and style according to the listeners, and Mila's songs were sung to a wide range of audiences. To peasants he met through his vow of begging only at the "first door" each day and to the rough, nomadic herdsmen he met in his wanderings, he sang of birth and death, the cause-effect relationship of action, impermanence, and ethical conduct in a simple and direct way, using everyday objects and experiences as his examples. For his own disciples he sang precise and pertinent instructions to open their minds for practice and to instruct and correct them. With disciples of other teachers, wandering yogis who would track him down for questioning and scholars eager to meet a person of real accomplishment, he was a master at assessing a person's stature and needs. For them he fashioned songs stunning with penetrating revelations. Among his audience were non-human demons, to whom he sang his challenges and warnings, and ḍākinīs, to whom he sang of his most secret and personal illuminations. A few times he met masters of comparable attainment. They traded teachings and challenges, miracles and revelations, in celebration of the spiritual achievements of their powerful, yogic minds.

Most of the pieces were sung in response to a question, challenge, or a request to sing for his supper. Milarepa responded not only to the questions, but also to the motivations behind them and the context in which they were asked. The songs invariably open with a line or verse of prayer to Marpa, Mila's lama, requesting his guidance and blessings, which for Mila and his followers had the power to improve and inspire their practice. Occasionally Mila would "supplicate" the buddhas and lamas on behalf of his listeners to direct them to Dharma or aid them in practice. When giving a teaching, he would often wrap it up with a string of concise exhortations called precepts. Most of the songs close with a dedication, or benediction, to share the merit of his practice with all beings and in particular to repay his patrons who had requested the song with an offering. Concerning the content and form of the individual songs translated in this volume, brief introductions precede each piece.

LET THIS FIRST SELECTION SERVE as an introduction to Milarepa himself. Here he's in the frequent situation of begging from some rather irritated villagers and is in an irascible mood himself: he's about to leave without giving the customary dedication of merit in return for his food when a monk's criticism prompts him to explain his own special yogic way of dedicating food and some of his personal history. Amazed by this unusually eloquent beggar, they ask about his identity. Mila responds with an account of his early life, his training, experiences, and realizations, and then teaches them about the samsaric condition and gives advice for their practice. This story also records his meeting with Wangchuk Dorje, who was to become one of Mila's regular disciples.

1

Milarepa Tells His Story

ONCE MILAREPA, THE GREAT LORD OF YOGIS, after spending the winter in the snows of Lachi Mountain, went in early summer to beg in the vicinity of Nyekha in Tsang. He entered a village and said to some people there, "We yogis have the vow of begging at the 'first door.' One of you faithful give us some food."

One patron responded, "I'll give you a rackful of fish meat." But Mila told him, "I don't eat the flesh of murdered beings."

"You don't eat the flesh of murdered beings! That's marvelous! I don't have any other food." He went away, but Mila remained where he was. Finally the patron came back with a bowlful of leftovers topped with yogurt, saying, "Oh well, you can eat this."

Mila ate it, and while he was preparing to leave, a monk who was there said, "Don't you know even one dedication or supplication? Can't you find even one overcoat? Where did you come from? Where are you going? If you know how, sing us a song."

So Jetsün sang this song:

> Precious true lama,
> Wishing gem whose mere memory's enough,
> I beg you with fervent devotion
> Grant your blessings to your devoted son.

> I've come from the slopes of Lachi Mountain
> Which stands in the region of Nyanang.
> Right now I've no set destination.

> I've never gathered any wealth;
> Like a beggar I take things as they come.
> When given food I do as follows:
> In this mansion which is the basis
> This illusory body made of four elements,

I transform elements, currents, channels, and drops
Into the inner deity which depends upon them.
I change into nectar whatever I eat;
And from the mouth of each deity
A hollow tongue of light extends.[10]

Like a reflection in a mirror—
Apparent yet insubstantial—
Deity makes offerings to deities.
Reality sports in the field of reality,
And on the state of freedom from addiction to concepts
I impress the seal of impartial dedication.
That's my way of dedicating food.

Sometimes in mountains empty of men
I survive on the food of mountain plants,
And my yoga of food is just like the above.

But mostly I eat the food of concentration,
My yoga of food and its dedication
Merged with the gnosis of nonidentification.
That's how I eat the food of secret practice.

Now I'll explain my way of dress:
In accord with the style of worldly men
I wrap myself in this one cotton cloth
And in accord with advanced beings
I survive by the inner warmth of gnosis.

Like lizards and toads
My skin is rough and green
And like baboons and monkeys
My body's covered with ash-gray hair.

Just like nettle-worms
My body's banded with dirt-crusted creases
And just like a baby's
My crotch lacks protection or covering.

In the manner of beggars
I find food like a bird,
And in a way I'm like the rich
With the wealth of inner satisfaction.

Like famished people
I leave no food for tomorrow,
And like madmen
I've no idea what to do or where to go.

Like the very wise
I hold fast to my human birthright,
And like idiots
I don't know about social conventions.

Like the greatest of teachers
I also know how to teach Dharma,
And like great snow lions
I too live in desolate mountains.

I take after gophers
And meditate in underground holes,
And like wild foxes
I live in gorges and canyons of mountains.

Like ancient sages
I've borne austerities a long time,
And like garuda birds
I soar through the vast expanse of the sky.

That explains my style of dress
And my way of doing yoga.
Now I'll sing a song of yoga,
For you said, "Sing a song! Sing a song!"
And this prattling gives me joy.

After leaving behind my homeland,
I took up practice in desolate mountains.
This mental ease and comfort of ear

Free from talk of taxes, debts, and armies
Was accomplished by myself, a beggar.
Wonderful—this blissful state of affairs!

I left behind my father's fine house,
And while practicing in mountain caves
I'd no need for repairs or patches in roofs.
This fine stone mansion of meditation
Was built by myself, a beggar.
Wonderful—this blissful state of affairs!

Leaving behind my father's rich field
I tamed the rough earth of my own mind.
This cultivation and pliability of mind,
This thorough perfection of love and compassion
Was accomplished by myself, a beggar.
Wonderful—this blissful state of affairs!

Lovers are trouble so I never married,
But attended the consort of clear light.
This union of method and wisdom,
This companionship of the natural state,
Was achieved by myself, a beggar.
Wonderful—this blissful state of affairs!

Away from troubles and confusion
I reared the infant of void awareness.
This resplendence of clear-light dharma-body
In unconditioned freedom from preconception
Was raised by myself, a beggar.
Wonderful—this blissful state of affairs!

I've never gathered worldly wealth
But relied on the wealth of satisfaction.
These seven superior treasures
Free from worries and vexation
Were acquired by myself, a beggar.
Wonderful—this blissful state of affairs!

I myself have achieved such joy;
If you think it's blissful, you should do likewise.
And there you have my song of yoga.

They were all overcome with awe and bowed to him, asking: "Great lord of yogis, where were you born? What's the name of your monastery? Who's your lama? Do you have any students? What's your name? Please tell us."

So Mila sang another song:

Lord of Dharma and savior of men—
To the feet of my merciful lama I bow.

Now then, you patrons gathered here,
I'll give brief answer to your questions.

My birthplace was the town of Kyanga Tsa
On Gungthang plain of Ngari Valley.
My father was Mila Sherab Gyentsen
And mother Nyangtsha Kargyen.
My own given name was Thöpa Ga,
And my sister's Peta Gonkyit.

While I was young my father died,
And bereft of wealth by evil relations
We three were forced to work as servants.
Wearing clothing tattered as fishnet
And fed like dogs, we slaved like mules.
My mother, driven by intense resentment,
Charged me to learn evil spells to destroy them,
But later I repented and turned to Dharma.

My lama is Marpa of Lhodrak.
As I had no wealth to give him
I offered the service of body, speech, and mind.
And by distilling the nectar of the all-profound precepts,
He gave me the most essential secrets of his mind.

So without a trace of laziness
I pursued the goal of reality

Till experience and realization were born in mind.

I've got several young student repas.
We stay in the mountains' perfect monastery,
Drinking the waters of austerity,
Eating nettles and mountain plants,
Or sometimes begging for our food.

My religious name is Dorje Gyentsen,
But I'm known as yogi Milarepa.
I go wherever I feel like going.
This is my answer to your questions.

The monk exclaimed, "I've heard of a siddha named Milarepa—you must
be that very same lama! Now I've seen you with my own eyes and heard you
with my own ears!" He prostrated himself and placed Mila's feet on his
head, then said, "Precious lama, at the end of your previous song you said,
'Like garuda birds I soar through the vast expanse of the sky.' I'm sure
you're not lying, but we could use a sure sign of your attainment."
So Mila sang:

Embodiment of great mercy,
All pervading dharma-body of clear light,
Universal lord unified with space—
To kind Marpa's feet I bow.

I the yogi Milarepa
Began meditation with fervent faith.
After initiation, empowerment, and instruction
I practiced with strong determination.

I entered retreat and did difficult practice
Till realization and experience were born in mind.
I realized the inner nature of samsara,
Saw the natural-state essence of mind,
Tore off the shackles of samsara,
And untied the knot of self-attachment.

Smothering the demon of belief in ego
And soaring in the vast sky free from addiction to concepts,
I saw without eyes the visible realm,
Heard without ears the sound of voidness,
Smelled without nose the natural state's scent,
Tasted without tongue reality's sweet taste,
Attained without body the rainbow vajra-body,
And was absorbed without mind in the mahāmudrā state.

Eh ma! The things of samsara's three realms
Don't exist—yet are just as they appear!
They appear—yet are voidness itself!
That's the nature of the illusion of the superficial world.

About the nature of reality I cannot speak—
An artist without hands
Draws pictures in the sky,
Without eyes sees myriad things
In perfect vision without movement or strain.

After singing this he rose into the air to a height of one story. The patron exclaimed in amazement, "Is this some kind of magic trick or optical illusion?" In reply Mila sang another song:

I bow to the feet of Lama Marpa
Who offered me buddhahood in the palm of his hand
By confronting me with reality
Through revelation of the natural state's nature.

Listen now, faithful patrons:
In the illusory city of samsara
Illusory men are completely confused;
They perform illusory actions in six states of existence.

Beings, the magical creations of action,
Ignorant of the working of such creation
Think they exist independent of creation,
But creation is essentially illusion.

Hey! Listen all you gathered here—
View mind and body in this way:
Mind is insubstantial, void awareness,
Body a bubble of flesh and blood.

If the two are indivisibly one,
Why would a corpse be left behind
At the time of death when consciousness leaves?
And if they are totally separate
Why would the mind experience pain
When harm happens to the body?

Thus, illusory appearances are the result
Of belief in the reality of the superficial,
Not knowing this action-caused conflux is illusion.

If you want to understand this illusion,
Serve a holy lama who's removed the illusion.
Practice holy Dharma which destroys illusion,
And realize the unillusory face of the mind.
When illusion's gone there's no confusion.

They were all overawed. Some passed out and saw a variety of visions. In particular, the monk was made ready for direct realization of the mind's natural state. Finally they asked him, "Precious lama, on the other side of this region there's a fine mountain retreat called Rich Woman's Pot. Please, your reverence, stay there from now on, or for a few years, or at least this summer and winter."

Mila said he would stay for the summer and left for Rich Woman's Pot. About fifteen people led by the monk and patron went with him. They all sought Dharma instruction and produced excellent realization by practicing. The monk himself was able to catch sight of the true goal. When he received profound Dharma empowerment, he was given the name Wangchuk Dorje. He later became a siddha.

Mila stayed for three months; they begged him to stay longer, but he didn't listen. They said, "If you absolutely refuse to grant our request and must leave us now, please give some advice about practice in the future of this life and the next."

So Mila sang them this song:

> Listen "great meditators," men and women:
> At best, you should do austere practice
> In desolate mountains for the rest of your lives.
> Next best is to wander the countryside,
> Impartial, directionless, detached from this life.
>
> Next best, follow me, unattached to your homeland,
> And at least until self-sufficient,
> Learn holy Dharma from a true lama—
> Experienced and realized—and remember key points.
>
> Avoid three faults of a pot[11] when listening to Dharma.
> Restrain body, speech, and mind and reflect on its meaning.
> Hang on well to the words that strike home.
> Stem the outbreak of afflictive emotions.
> Make fruitful the holy Dharma you've heard.
>
> About the things of this life think as follows—
> About involvement in all the complex affairs
> Of politics and government think thus:
>
> Desires achieved increase thirst like salt water.
> Work has no end like a river's ripples.
> Prosperity and decline are like a pond's filling and drying.
>
> These preconceived obsessive emotions
> Are a curtain which hides high birth and freedom,
> An iron hook dragging us to low birth in samsara,
> The seeds of repeated growth of afflictions,
> A massive cloud raining down mystery,
> A thief who robs our virtue and assets,
> The root that produces all of our faults.
>
> To probe deep into your roots:
> The ignorance and confusion are you yourself.
> The preconceptions which are yourself
> Are envoys and agents sent by yourself.

From beginningless time till now you've dragged yourself
Through the mire of bad actions in samsara's ocean.

Now examine yourself closely:
You yourself have no color or form.
If sent you won't go.
If restrained you don't stay.
If looked for you can't be seen.
If grasped for you can't be caught.

Previously ignorant of your own nature,
You spun on the wheel of affliction in the ocean of life.
Now, in the mansion of concentration and physical composure,
Examine before you with eyes of critical awareness
And station behind the watchman of recollective awareness.
Return to your natural state without effort or distraction.
Know the way of such relaxation, fortunate ones.

Mila then left for Lachi Mountain accompanied by Wangchuk Dorje and several others, and there they practiced.

THE PREVIOUS STORY is a model of Milarepa's history and teachings as told to peasant audiences, covering a wide range of material he commonly taught them. The next two pieces are peasant stories also and expand on some of the themes presented in the opening story: samsara and its frustrations, impermanence, and the triumph of Mila's own yogic lifestyle.

2

Song for Poor Patrons

AGAIN, WHILE JETSÜN WAS STAYING at Red Block Rock a patron named Auspicious Fortune came to meet him. After offering respects to Mila he said, "Father, precious Jetsün, you have lived in desolate mountain retreats with no regrets. Now, while engaged day and night in generating the profound mental power to provide for the welfare of beings, consider us, the people of Dam Valley, with compassion. We have poor faith and no opportunity to practice. We're completely involved in the affairs of this life. We are paupers lacking even enough flour to make torma offerings. Please focus your profound mental power on us and, though we have no way to make the proper offerings, teach us one session of Dharma to plant the seeds of liberation through your compassionate vision."

So Jetsün taught them Dharma about the cause and effect relationship of action and afterwards sang this song:

> I pray to the translator renowned
> Named Marpa Lotsawa,
> Excellent man of Lhodrag
> With the precious power of speaking two tongues.
>
> I, Milarepa, well nourished
> By my holy lama's kindness,
> Don't know much about worldly affairs;
> But when I stay in mountains empty of men—
> Stores of food and wealth left ungathered—
> Faithful patrons, men and women,
> Gather like a swarm of bees
> On a sweet-smelling lotus blossom.
>
> All this is my lama's kindness—
> Pray grant me your constant blessings.
>
> I, Mila of the mountain retreats,
> Don't engage in business or trade;

But while I'm living on desolate mountains,
Not relying on alms to subsist,
Faithful patrons, men and women,
Bring me delicious food and drink.

All this is my lama's kindness.
I offer worship to repay that kindness—
Pray grant me your constant blessings!

I, Mila of the mountain retreats,
Don't rely on the food of circle feasts
Or on the essences of yogic pills;[12]
But when I live in desolate mountain retreats
Faithful patrons, men and women,
Supply me with ambrosial drink.

All this is my lama's kindness.
I offer worship to repay that kindness—
Pray grant me your constant blessings!

I, yogi-repa of the mountains,
Don't want fine, soft silken clothes
From desire for impressiveness or beauty;
But when I'm living in mountains empty of men
Faithful patrons, men and women,
Provide me with good woolen robes.

All this is my lama's kindness.
I offer worship to repay that kindness—
Pray grant me your constant blessings.

These were all external matters,
Now I'll tell my inner story:

When I practice as instructed
By my true and holy lama,
Having offered him body, speech, and mind,
Blessings and accomplishments fall like rain,
And bliss-warmth of experience glows in my body.

This is the best way of serving a ruler—
I've left all worldly rulers behind.

When I concern myself with the things at hand
And shoulder the burden of austerities,
Worldly affairs are all forgotten.
Such direct influence on the four elements
And sustenance by the food of absorption
Are the best of all means of nourishment—
I've left worldly food and drink behind.

When I drink at the stream of enlightenment,
Or the cool blue waters of a mountain cascade,
Which is the property of no one else,
Strong tea and beer are both abandoned.
Such easing of the pain of affliction
Is the best way of taking drink—
I've left tea and beer behind.

When I develop my currents, channels, and such,
Wearing only the cotton robe of repas,
Clothes of the great, silk of nobility,
And fine, soft wool are all abandoned.
Such warm burning bliss of *tummo*
Is the best way of wearing clothes—
I've left fine silken cloth behind.

When I make my home in mountain caves,
Great mansions and troublesome environs
Of homeland are abandoned.
Such a fine mansion of absorption
And homeland of mental stability
Is the best way of taking abode—
I've left homeland and fine houses behind.

When I cultivate the friendship of wisdom,
I abandon the problems
Of an ever-troublesome mate.
Such integration of method and wisdom

Firmly based on love and compassion
Is the best kind of companionship—
I've left the problems of marriage behind.

When I nourish the infant of clear light,
I abandon the quarrels of inimical children
Who in return for their loving care
Are the main trouble of their parents' old age.
Such relationship of mother-reality and child
Put to rest in the natural state's cradle
Is the best way of raising offspring—
I've left the misfortune of dear children behind.

When I rely on the seven superior treasures,[13]
I abandon attraction, aversion, and strife
For the sake of wealth which binds to samsara.
Such wealth of knowing all things as illusion
And of realizing what is sufficient
Is the best way of amassing treasure—
I've left all worldly wealth behind.

When I subdue the enemy egoism
And hold fast to humility,
I've left the land where the three poisons are born.
Such freedom from inimical afflictions
Through realization that all beings are our parents
Is the best way of taming enemies—
I've left the fighting of worldly foe behind.

When I press toward the goal of reality,
I read the path of the six transcendences
And guide with the four social means
Relations who've lovingly nursed me
Throughout the beginningless space of samsara.
This is the best mind of relationship—
I've left worldly relationships behind.

When I work for freedom of all beings, our mothers,
With the good intent of enlightenment mind,

Such varied work for the welfare of beings
By showing them the vehicles' stages
Suited to the mental needs of each
Is the best of all kinds of friendship—
I've left worldly friendships behind.

That was my inner story—
Now I'll tell my secret story:

In the face of reality's illumination
There is neither self nor other,
No duality, no division—void of identity
And yet neither void
Nor not void,
There's no perceiver at all.
Eh Ma! Until a mountain yogi
Has realized well the meaning of this,
He should not disparage cause and result!

May you patrons, men and women gathered here,
Have the fortune of long life, no sickness,
With enjoyment of perpetual bliss.

May you have the fortune of dharma-body in the face of death,
And the fortune of realizing buddha-body in your body,
Buddha-speech in your speech,
And buddha-mind in your mind.
May you have the fortune of the three bodies
Spontaneously achieved with body, speech, and mind.
Singing this auspicious song of experience
In this auspicious mountain retreat,
Consider, Auspicious Fortune, the host of ḍākinīs
Auspiciously assembled here
And a multitude of the fortunate
Worshipping them with auspicious song.

Overcome with powerful emotion, the patrons provided him with service and requested him to stay. This song belongs to the first series of songs sung while he lived at Red Block Rock.

Girl offering butter

3

Mila's Song in the Rain

ONCE WHILE JETSÜN WAS STAYING in Pelma Gel cave he went begging at a large encampment. A young patroness paid respects and offered a small piece of butter. Remembering that he had already received his daily share of food, he said, "I don't even have a container to hold this butter; keep it yourself."

The woman was impressed and asked him to stay for the day. He did so, sitting a little way off. A torrential rain fell, and she said to him, "Oh my, let me pitch a tarp overhead."

Mila replied with this song:

> I bow at the feet of the jewel crowning my head,
> Holy fulfiller of all wants and needs.
>
> Gracious woman blessed with offspring and wealth
> Managing an abundant treasury of gifts,
> Clothed in the woolen robe of merit—
> Listen here, faithful lady.
>
> If you don't know my name,
> I'm Milarepa of Gungthang plain—
> A beggar wandering by myself.
> Moved by my suffering from cold wind and rain,
> You offered this help in true spirit of mercy.
> Such good intentions are indeed a great wonder.
>
> I've traveled the plains of six illusory realms
> Where a rain of misery fell without pause
> And the dark fog of delusion pressed close around me.
>
> I lacked the broad hat of right view,
> The raincoat of unfaltering faith,
> And the warm dry cave of good refuge.

Swept by the river of desire and craving
Swollen by driving rains of bad action,
I was borne to the horizon of the ocean of misery,
Buffeted on waves of three lower realms,
And battered on rocks of unwholesome action.

In fear of such insufferable miseries
In future lives beyond number,
I pitched the white tent of right view
On the great plain of unfaltering faith.

I tied the tent ropes of meditative experience,
Drove in the tent pegs of unerring practice,
Erected the poles of resultant three bodies,
And hoisted the banner of pure behavior.

I broadcast the holy Dharma drumbeat to all directions,
And on the throne of manifold objective world
Imbibe the broth of all profound precepts.

On the great plateau of love and compassion
I herd the six realms' sheep from the edge
And gather the nectar of omniscient gnosis
Unobstructed toward all objects.

Blissful within, I don't entertain
The notion "I'm suffering"
When incessant rain is pouring outside.

Even on peaks of white snow mountains
Amidst swirling snow and sleet
Driven by new year's wintry winds
This cotton robe burns like fire.

The young woman was inspired with strong faith. That evening she requested blessings and initiation, offering an elaborate circle feast. All the other people of that encampment also came seeking religious association with Jetsün. They made many offerings, but he didn't accept them, singing this song:

I pray to the feet of my kind lama.
All the food and drink you've taken
Through beginningless samsara
Till this present life
Hasn't given you satisfaction or fulfillment.
Eat therefore this food
Of good concentration, fortunate ones.

All the wealth you've acquired
From beginningless time until now
Has failed to fulfill all your desires.
Cultivate therefore this wish-granting gem
Of moderation, fortunate ones.

All friends you've known
From beginningless time till now
Have never remained by your side.
Keep therefore the lasting company
Of primordial mahāmudrā, fortunate ones.

Knowing hoarded possessions will be left behind,
I don't crave a rich man's wealth,
And therefore I don't want your offerings.

May you live long lives, happy and healthy,
Free from misery and untimely death,
And take rebirth in a buddha's pure land.

Mila then left for Red Block Rock of Gungthang Plain.

A YOGI HAS COME to find out about the man whose reputation has been spreading throughout Tibet. Thus Mila's first song concerns the misleading nature of name and fame. The yogi is troubled at seeing the lonely, austere condition under which Mila preferred to practice—extreme even for practitioners of his time. Mila sings him a song of yogic fearlessness and a song of precepts—short, pithy statements that are like keys to understanding and practice. Here they are concerned with the naturally liberated nature of the apparent world and the way of removing the deluded preconceptions that compel us to misperceive the world as we ordinarily do. Although it's not mentioned, these precepts refer to the practice of mahāmudrā and are precise directions.

4

Mila Meets a Yogi

ONE WARM DAY while the great Jetsün Repa was practicing at Red Block Rock on Gungthang plain, a yogi arrived. Mila asked him, "Where are you coming from?"

He replied, "I've come from the region of Ü after hearing the fame of a Jetsün lama named Milarepa. Where is this holy Jetsün living?"

In reply Mila sang him this song:

> I bow to the feet of Marpa, best of men,
> Inseparable from great Vajradhara.
> Pray direct me, your mind undeflected
> From the state of changeless reality.
>
> You, ascetic of Ü, visiting from the lowlands,
> Seek out yogi Mila for teachings.
> Understand, then, this explanation!
>
> In the three spring months when the king of warmth appears
> And the elements of heat and cold contend,
> The sound "ur-ur" reverberates in the sky,
> And is called Blue Dragon.
>
> Though name and fame are great,
> When his *real form* is encountered,
> He has large mouth, thin neck, long tail.
>
> Though name and form don't agree,
> His voice is considered most auspicious.
> Thus he's called great dragon of the sky,
> Divider of summer and winter,
> And pearl of timely rainfall.
> Understand this is a great wonder!

Beneath the currents of the outer ocean's waters,
Upon the ocean's golden dais,
Sits the lord of the ocean
Called Great Golden Tortoise.

Though name and fame are great,
When his real form is encountered
He's like a clay pot turned upside down
With big mouth, short legs.

Though name and form don't agree,
He's called Great Golden Tortoise.
He's the great ornament of the oceans,
Medicine for taming elemental spirits,
Weapon guarding the evil regions,
And conqueror of evil serpents.
Understand this is a great wonder!

Here in Tibet red-faced demons,
Yakshas, and a host of spirits
Are seeking any opportunity for harm.
It's I who is renowned as Milarepa;
And though name and fame are great,
When my real form is encountered,
I am naked, body green.

Though name and form don't agree,
I've the ability to practice austere Dharma;
Thus I'm the crown of Dharma-seekers,
A yogi who upholds the teachings
With the strength to conquer spirits and demons.
Understand this is a great wonder!

These three—song, example, and meaning,
Are Mila's way of explanation;
But actually this Milarepa
Is just name, just symbol and designation—
Empty like chaff, insubstantial,
Essenceless—thus I have no teaching.

This is my offering to you, yogi.
Do you get my meaning, ascetic?

Filled with admiration, the yogi bowed, circled Mila and then knelt with folded hands. "I didn't know it was you at first. Forgive me. I'm amazed that you're able to stay in this desolate retreat without fear, worry, or anxiety."

Jetsün replied, "If a yogi is afraid to stay in mountain retreats, he hasn't even tasted the scent of yoga. You must identify the goal, which is the natural state, by learning and thinking. Then, after receiving the profound precepts from a real lama and cutting off mental fabrication, realize the aim of one-pointed meditation. Such a person should be called 'yogi.' Those who go wandering around the country without the authority of experience and realization, begging food and doing whatever they please, are persons overcome by evil. Therefore, listen and consider well this song of mine."

> Dharma-lord of unwavering kindness,
> Translator whose name is rare to hear—
> To the great translator Marpa
> I pray—grant me blessings!
>
> When great mahāmudrā is manifested,
> A yogi doesn't fear even destruction of this illusory body.
> Just realizing that inner and outer experiences are illusions
> A yogi doesn't fear even the armies of the four devils.
>
> When he has slashed his attachment to life,
> A yogi doesn't fear even the three realms' total destruction.
> When he's able to reverse the bodhicitta[14] in the yoni
> A yogi isn't afraid to wander the three realms' fog.

The yogi was overwhelmed and exclaimed, "Precious Jetsün Lama, you have a great reputation, and it's truly so. Wonderful! Wonderful! Now, please explain how this apparent world appears."

So Mila sang this song:

> I bow at the feet of the true lama
> Who showed me that appearances are illusion.

Do you know what these appearances are?
If you don't know, I'll tell you:
These appearances appear everywhere;
For the unrealized they are samsara,
But they shine for the realized as dharma-body.
When appearances shine as dharma-body
Don't seek a view from other sources.

Do you know how to cultivate mind?
If you don't know, I'll tell you:
Don't attempt to manipulate mind;
Don't try to force control of mind.
Relax like a young child.
Be like a waveless ocean.
Like a self-illuminating lamp,
And like a lifeless corpse.
Clear the mind of exaggeration.

Do you know how to experience?
If you don't know, I'll tell you:
Just as fog is dispelled by the strength of the sun
And is dispelled no other way,
Preconception is cleared by the strength of realization.
There's no other way of clearing preconceptions.
Experience them as baseless dream.
Experience them as ephemeral bubbles.
Experience them as insubstantial rainbow.
Experience them as indivisible space.

Do you know how to amend experience?
If you don't know, I'll tell you:
Even a strong wind is empty by nature.
Even a great wave is just ocean itself.
Even thick southern clouds are insubstantial as sky.
Even the dense mind is naturally birthless.
To set the mind in motion
Use precepts for mounting consciousness on currents.

When losing to the thief, preconception,
Use precepts for recognizing the thief.
When mind is scattered to objects
Employ the precept of the raven's flight from a boat.[15]

Do you know how to practice?
If you don't know, I'll tell you:
Practice like a great lion stands.
Practice like a lotus growing in mud.
Practice like an infatuated elephant.
Practice like a clear crystal ball.

Do you know how to manifest results?
If you don't know, I'll tell you:
Dharma-body is manifested in preconceptionlessness.
Enjoyment-body is manifested in bliss.
Emanation-body is manifested in clarity.
Essential-body is manifested in primal void.
For those skilled in words there are three bodies,
But in dharma-body there are no divisions.

View, cultivation, experience,
Emendation, practice, and results—
These six comprise yogic experience.
Do you get my meaning, man of Ü?
Do you understand me, ascetic?

The yogi was again overwhelmed, and after requesting initiation and profound instruction began his practice. He is said to have become an expert meditator through the dawning of ultimate realization in his mind.

ANOTHER YOGIC SONG, this time sung for Milarepa's own close disciple Rechungpa. It is a good example of the way Mila styled his yogic teachings for his own disciples. This spontaneous outpouring in response only to the request of Rechungpa's folded hands, reflects these relaxed circumstances in the unity and proportions of its form. Using the kind of metaphorical style he liked, Mila takes objects in his immediate surroundings and weaves them into a rich symbolic fabric illustrating essential points of his teaching.

5

Symbols for Yogic Experience

AFTER HAVING MADE THEIR WINTER HOME at Lachi, Jetsün Milarepa and several disciples went up to Gungthang plain for the summer, staying in White Rock Horse Tooth Cave.

One day Mila and Rechungpa walked to upper Yerpo to refresh their bodies. Rechungpa silently addressed his lama with folded hands and they both sat down for a while.

Vultures soared above them. Grouse called to their right. Alert deer grazed on grass to their left while their young played. And below them a rushing cascade plunged into the Tsangpo River.

Seeing this Mila was delighted and sang this song:

I bow to the feet of my revered lama.

Listen son, Rechung Dorje Drak,
These vultures, our neighbors, king of birds,
Vultures soaring in the sphere of the sky,
Seek their food on these three mountain peaks,
And on the side of Red Rock take their rest.

All these are symbols of yogic sight:
This sight without circumference or center.
The vulture of voidness-realization
Compassionately dives for the food of other's welfare
And sleeps on the rock of ultimate unification.

Blissful are yogis devoted wholly to Dharma.
Do you get my meaning, Rechungpa?
In considering this our minds become happy.

These grouse, our neighbors, godlike birds,
Call sweetly from thickets of mountain river,
Search for fruits in alpine meadows,
And in the rooks of Clay Rock take their sleep.

All these are symbols of yogic meditation:
This gracious bird of the natural meditative state
Calls sweetly with the voice of primal being,
Feeds in the grass of quiescence unwavered,
And sleeps in the state of self-illumined insight.

Blissful the yogi arrived at mind's true essence.
Do you get my meaning, Rechungpa?
In considering this our minds become happy.

These watchful deer, our neighbors,
Leave these three barren mountain peaks
And descend to graze in meadow pastures.
There they play in conditions of comfort,
And by Mighty Rock take their sleep.

All these are symbols of yogic practice:
This spontaneous freedom encountered in practice
Is alertness balancing experience good and bad.
It descends to the meadows of love and compassion,
Sports with the welfare of all sentient beings,
And keeps close to the rock of dedication impartial.

Blissful the yogi whose mind is alert.
Do you get my meaning, Rechungpa?
In considering this our minds become happy.

Our drinking water, this cool mountain river,
Springs up by itself in the meadows of White Rock,
Fills up the hollow of Clay Rock,
And flows on unbroken through the three valleys' junction.

All these are symbols of yogic results:
These results, the self-sufficient buddha bodies,
Arise on their own as results on the basis,
Fill up the hollow of pure supplication,
And fulfill others' welfare till the end of existence.

Blissful the yogi who's free of anxiety.
Do you get my meaning, Rechungpa?
In considering this our minds become happy.

In White Rock Cave, my place of practice,
I produce the force of concentration beyond meditation.
Warriors and ḍākinīs collect like a cloud
As I spend the night watchful, in blissful awareness,
Replete with all sorts of auspicious omens.
Daytime, realization shines as blissful experience;
Meditating thus, I'm a Great Meditator Repa.

Toss to the winds your concern for this life,
And impress on your mind the unknown time of your death.
Remembering the pain of samsara,
Why long for the unnecessary?

Spend human life in the egoless valley,
Hold fast to the seat of courage unbending,
And fulfill the interests of yourself and others.

Do you get my meaning, Rechungpa?
Mila has considered this and his mind is happy.

I offer this song of worship, revered lama!
Share in this feast of sound, host of ḍākinīs!
Remove your obstructions, nonhumans!
Attend this auspicious song of worship!

THE ULTIMATE GUIDE is one's own self; or more explicitly, it is the way the experiences of one's life and practice are understood and utilized to best advantage. That's the only real indication of where one is and where to head. Mila's students want to make a pilgrimage to a famous shrine, so Mila points out the irrelevance of such formalities and explains what is important.

6

Song of the Path Guides

JETSÜN STAYED WITH FIVE OF HIS DISCIPLES in White Rock Horse Tooth Cave until cool autumn weather arrived. The young repas asked their lama, "Now it's autumn. Shouldn't we gather provisions for winter practice by begging supplies? By doing so we would help those beings gain merit. And also, it would be a joy to visit the statue of the Precious Lord Buddha in Kyirong.[16] Please let us go."

The lama replied to them, "The 'Precious Lord' is complete within yourselves. And also, it's not so fine for yogis to be begging food. Therefore, take up the practice of these eight vajra paths." And he sang this song for the young repas in White Rock Horse Tooth Cave:

> Glorious incarnation of universal ruler,
> Best cure for the sickness of the three poisons,
> Excellent man of Lhodrak—
> To Marpa the translator I bow!
>
> White Rock Horse Tooth, fortress of the middle way,
> Gathering place for noble ḍākinīs,
> Place inspiring sincere faith in the old,
> Practice site of the confident—
>
> In this best of retreats
> Receive a song of the natural-state experience.
> Hear this song, five brother repas—
> My children Lodro, Shergön Dorje, and others.
> The eternal, changeless fundamental consciousness
> Is the path guide to freedom from samsara.
> Happy is one who knows samsara and nirvana are not two;
> Wondrous the cultivation of this crop!
>
> This holy, true lama
> Is the path guide for clearing the darkness of ignorance.

Happy is one who sees lama as buddha;
Wondrous this ceaseless admiration and faith!

This mountain retreat without direction
Is the path guide for nourishing concentration.
Happy is one who treats the body as retreat;
Wondrous this immutable abiding!

This objective world appearing to the senses
Is the path guide for cultivating spontaneous awareness.
Happy is one who's directed them to the central channel;
Wondrous this pervasion of body and mind by bliss!

These precepts for transference of consciousness
Are path guides for overcoming the visions of bardo.
Happy is one who can cross with awareness;
Wondrous this conflux of past, present, and future!

The precious embodiments of love and compassion
Are path guides for impartial help for beings.
Happy is one surrounded by the realized;
Wondrous this help by emanation-body for beings!

This cultivation of pure, undistracted absorption
Is the path guide for refining awareness.
Happy is one who knows the actual as nondual;
Wondrous this awareness pure as space!

This cotton robe upon your body
Is the path guide for mastering these harsh snow mountains.
Happy is one who sleeps naked in snow;
Wondrous this freedom from heat and cold!

This song I sing of eight vajra paths
Is itself a path guide self-voiced like echo.
Happy the yogi who remembers this song of experience;
Wondrous this self-voiced vajra sound.

I offer this song of worship, holy lama!
Share in this feast of sound, host of ḍākinīs!
Remove your obstructions, nonhumans!
Attend this auspicious song of worship!

As he sang, flowers fell from the sky and a never-before-experienced per-
fume was smelled. Each of the five disciple-repas experienced a different
vision. Together they paid respects and offered a mandala (*maṇḍala*) with
the fervent request that Mila remain with them. Inspired by such uncon-
trollable faith, favorable meditation experiences were kindled in them, and
they made renewed effort in practice.

MILA DEDICATES this spontaneous song of realization to all meditators. He opens with a passage dealing with the practice of quiescence and analytic insight. After an ecstatic statement describing the mental development he's gained from such practice, Mila closes with a set of admonitions in precept form.

7

Song of Experience in Clear Light Cave

JETSÜN MILAREPA LEFT White Rock Horse Tooth Cave and returned again to the Clear Light Cave of Gungthang. While he was staying there, clear illumination grew stronger in his concentrated mind and he sang this song:

Homage to my holy lama!

I, the yogi Milarepa,
Offer my experience and realization
To all meditators of the ten directions.

My mind is relaxed in its natural state
Without rigidity or tension
Through gentle, undistracted cultivation.

I look straight ahead with the eye of critical awareness,
Station behind the watchman of recollective awareness,
And hold body and mind comfortably alert.

My mind rests in its natural state
Unaffected by drowsiness or mental sinking,
The aberrations of my mind's eye
And the various experiences during quiescence
Dissolved and sent back to their natural place.

In the experience of thought-free quiescence
The clear mind possesses its own force,
Naked—limpid and pure.
This is correct quiescence experience.
Some claim this is *insight*,
But I don't agree.[17]

So upon the horse of good quiescence
I mount awareness which comprehends

The selflessness of both persons and things
Through fine inspection by analytic wisdom.

Carrying as provisions my lama's blessings,
Which were sought with plaintive prayer,
I'm accompanied by wisdom and method
With personalities of voidness and compassion.

Driven on by the profound, great iron goad
Of strongly motivated good wishes,
I look again and again at basic reality
With gentle, undistracted cultivation
Free from hope and from despair.

Know that having traveled this good meditation path
I see it now with insight.
Know I've arrived in the untraveled country;
Know I have flour without grinding.

Know that I watch the unseen spectacle.
Know that I've found an auspicious homeland.
Know that I've found a constant consort.
Know I provide welfare for myself and others.

These are the treasures of Milarepa;
If I'm on the wrong path, please set me straight.

Eh ma! Till you practitioners of the ten directions
Attain perfect buddhahood
Don't deny cause and effect of action!
Till you've realized the actual state
Don't make senseless, empty talk!

Till you're able to exchange your interests with others'
Don't say, "I've obtained the enlightenment-mind."

Till your body's reflected as deity's body
Don't say, "I've attained the production stage!"

74

Till both stages are attained
Don't say, "I'm a yogi of secret mantras!"

While quiescence experience is still jumbled
And illusory appearances in dream confused,
Don't give out meaningless prophesies
Claiming to have supernormal perception.

Strong confidence in the lama's precepts sprang up in his disciples. They made renewed efforts in undistracted practice of the profound river-like current of yoga.

THIS PIECE CENTERS ON THE NATURE of analytic insight and the transcendent wisdom it generates. Rechungpa's meditation has been upset by a series of overwhelming hallucinations. He was able to recognize that they were induced by the force of his meditation and apply corrective measures, but faced with the nihilistic hallucination of utter nothingness, he was helpless. This is a common experience: illusions that are materialistic misperceptions are easier to deal with than those erring on the nihilistic side.

Mila tells in yogic terms exactly what had occurred—that such experiences are concomitant with Rechungpa's positive developments—and then explains the essential point; that transcendent gnosis involves realization of the nonduality of subject and object. The mind is incapable of truly seeing itself; its nature can be realized only through the elimination of preconceived misperceptions of the mind and its objects. The ordinary, mundane mind interprets experience in terms of verbal conventions, the conceptual consensus of the world determined before birth and subsequently elaborated by the conditionings of deluded experience. The direct experience of voidness is the perception of a lack—the inherent lack of independent identity in any thing. It is arrived at through the systematic elimination of mistaken assumptions that interpret the world as something more or something less than it actually is. No identity exists, yet the manifold phenomena of the subjective and objective worlds appear—that's the realization at the end of the meditational process of analysis.

8

Rechungpa's Confusion

ONE MORNING WHILE THE JETSÜN LAMA and his "son" Rechungpa were staying in the great cave of Red Block Rock, Rechungpa approached him. After paying respects many times, he knelt with folded hands and said:

I praise Jetsün's embodiment:
Naked body endowed with lustre,
Voice proclaiming sweet, ceaseless vajra-sound,
Mind absorbed in the pure realm of reality.

I, Rechungpa Dorje Drak,
Born in upper Gungthang plain
Obtained human birth by accumulated merit
And encountered you, glorious savior of beings.

Guided by your great compassion
I began the process of profound path teachings.
I sought *tummo* teaching in particular,
And when slight experience and realization dawned,
You revealed to me the ultimate.
Conviction of view was born within,
And I obtained unshakable faith.

Jetsün, you told me then,
"All the magic-like experiences that occur
Are magical creations of mind.
Come to the primordial reality state."

This is what occurred:
I strayed from naturally lucid awareness
And fell under sway of mental illusions.

Sometimes hallucinations of earth occurred:
During fearsome events like entrapments, landslides, and rock falls,

I focused myself on their true nature,
And the flow of manifold thought-forms shone
As luminosities of lustrous, golden light.

Sometimes hallucinations of water occurred:
I was swept away by swift, rushing waters
And tossed about on the waves of great oceans—
And they shone as dark blue luminosities.

Sometimes hallucinations of fire occurred:
Tongues of flame flickered; I fell into an inferno,
Enveloped in swirling red-black flame and smoke—
And they shone as fiery luminosities.

But other times by great roaring winds,
I was blown into the dark-lit realm of space
And rocked to and fro with soft, rushing sound.
With no reference point in mind
I was struck with dread of utter nothing.

When such consuming hallucinations occurred
Meditation faltered and went astray.
How should I handle this?
Merciful lama, please speak.

In reply Mila sang:

With respectful body, speech, and mind
I pray to great translator Marpa
Who set me on the nonillusory path
By smashing apart the cage of illusion.

Listen now, Rechungpa:
Sometimes when focusing on the reality state
Hallucinations of earth are experienced,
And likewise water, fire, wind, and space.
Because of them panic strikes,
The naturally lucid colors of the elements shine,
And manifold magic-like creations appear.

This body was acquired from action
Accumulated by ignorance through beginningless time,
The principal functioning mind *itself*
In turn planting seeds of ignorant action
In the ground of the fundamental consciousness.

Through beginningless time till now
You've been lost on the vast plain of illusion
In illusory bodies composed this way.

Now by lama's precepts
Your mind was squeezed a bit,
And these painful hallucinations experienced
Through slight penetration of your channels' mouths
By the four elements—
The sign of slight loosening of knotted channels
And stirring of currents and white element.

Why be unhappy or fearful
Or panicked by this?
It's the painful sign of positive practice,
A slight bit of meditation experience,
The sign of opening the channels' mouths,
The revelation of the four elements' lustre.

Now here's your lama's precept on this,
The exhortation of his pointing finger—
Bear it in mind, noble son!

If you wish the vision of real gnosis,
Investigate the nature of mind
With mind in this way:

This Mind-in-itself clear and void,
Like space is free of any thing;
No way at all exists
To make it an object of its own cognition.

This is, for example, like the inability

Of an eye to see itself,
Or of space to reveal
Its own unrevealable nature.

Mind cannot see itself—
Subject and object *cannot* be dual;
Therefore, to see the mind
You must look and probe with the eye of wisdom.

When probed and examined analytically
With such analytic investigation
The mind is like the wick of a lamp
Illumined only through its own radiance.

Likewise, though this natural, self-illumined mind
Is clear and free from obscuration,
It is born and dies through cause and effect
In every moment of awareness
And can know itself only through analysis.
What then is the mode of such realization?

During realization of voidness by nondual awareness,
Blissful, clear, and free from thought-flow,
Even *this* realization by such awareness
Free from duality of subject and object,
Of knower and known,
Is just a verbal convention.
Know that verbal conventions
Are not seen to exist
Subjectively, objectively, or in combination.

To sum it up, it's like this:
This fundamental consciousness
In itself is nothing at all.
In the voidness of reality
Lack of realizer and realized is realized,
Lack of seer and seen is seen,
Lack of knower and known is known,
Lack of perceiver and percept is perceived.

Thus, by slashing your confused assumptions from within
By realizing, seeing, knowing, and perceiving
The nonexistence of any center in mind,
Understand that all those appearances—
The manifold transformations of mind—
Are of one taste in the voidness of reality.

In voidness there's no excess or lack—
No appearance, disappearance, or change.
This reality of the mind-itself aware,
Though it appears as the conflux of many mistakes,
Is essentially free from birth or death,
Of coming or going, or change.
There's no excess or lack, no fullness or decay,
No help or harm, no existence or nonexistence at all.

This fundamental consciousness of the mind-itself
Has no original foundation,
No creative cause or condition.
For its duration there's nothing to be clarified
In its ephemeral mental functionings;
And in the end no cessation.

This utterly clear analytic awareness,
Indistinguishable from the vastness of space,
Is but a unitary thing,
Yet by conditions for objects the many appear;
Many appear, yet are but one—
And in that one no identity perceived.

Opening the door on voidness of identity,
Clear awareness floods everywhere,
And though everywhere, nowhere is an identity found.

Though no identity exists in the state of reality,
Fleeting illusions flash through mind.
Though manifold mistakes occur,
No base or root in them can be grasped.

Cultivate this mergence into the natural state
Through thorough investigation
By analytic wisdom.

Thus today I've imparted to my son
This fatherly advice;
After realizing its ultimate import,
May you have the fortune of guiding
All living beings to freedom.

PHADAMPA SANGYE, AN INDIAN MASTER of unusual accomplishments, reached Tibet in 1092. He is cited in chapter 30 of the *Hundred Thousand Songs* as one of five enlightened yogis of the time. He was a disciple of the Indian siddhas Nāgārjuna and Virūpa and belonged to the tantric school of Vikramaśīla Monastery. The lineage of his teachings, called "Pacification of Misery" (Tib. *sdug bsngal zhi byed*) did not survive as an independent system, as he predicts in this story. However, he also brought the "Severance" (Tib. *gcod*) teachings to Tibet and Nepal and taught the famous Nepali yoginī Ma Chig Lab Drön (Tib. *ma gcig lab sgron*) who created her own special form of "Severance." The Severance system did continue intact up to the present and is the only lineage to have returned to India after development in Tibet.

This story includes two well-known songs—Mila's "Crazy Song" and "Song of Fearlessness"—both contained in the *Hundred Thousand Songs*. Phadampa Sangye's last precepts to the people of Dingri, the town in southwestern Tibet where he had founded a monastery and which was frequented by Mila himself, are contained in *The Tibetan Book of the Great Liberation*.

9

Mila's Meeting with Dampa Sangye

ONCE THE INDIAN MASTER PHADAMPA SANGYE had the thought, "That Tibetan Milarepa is said to be an excellent siddha. I must meet him at least once." So he flew from India at daybreak and arrived at the top of Thongla Pass in Nyanang at the first direct rays of the sun. There he multiplied himself into the forms of many masters identical to himself and sat in their midst.

Meanwhile Mila, traveling from the base of Dingri plateau in the company of some traders, met him at the top of the pass. Identifying Dampa as the one with humble demeanor in the midst of all the masters, Jetsün offered his respects.

The master said, "There's no one here more lowly than me. Don't honor me senselessly. You must be crazy, yogi."

Mila answered with this song:

> To my omniscient lama I pray—
> Grant me blessings.
>
> Indian yogi, listen please:
> Afflicted by the devil of ignorance
> Most beings of the six realms are crazy.
> Having realized appearances to be illusory
> Milarepa especially is crazy.
>
> With supernormal knowledge of others' minds
> Old father Marpa Lotsawa is crazy.
> With courage in hardships for the sake of Dharma
> Grandfather, great pandit Nāropa, is crazy.
> With inconceivable powers of transformation
> Great-grandfather Tilo Sherab Sangbo is crazy.
>
> Granting the gift of spontaneous bliss
> Vajrayoginī is also crazy.
> Embraced in untainted union of great bliss

Lineage-source Vajradhara is crazy.

Attempting to hide yourself from me
Honorable Dampa—you're crazy too!
Your father's crazy, son's crazy, grandfather's crazy!
You're crazy, I'm crazy, everyone's crazy!

Some are crazed by ignorant action.
Some are crazed by the river of desire.
Some are crazed by the fire of hatred.
Some are crazed by the fog of delusion.
Some are crazed by the poison of pride.

You're crazed from knowing others' minds.
I'm crazed from realizing the natural state.

You're crazed by seed-syllable realization.
I'm crazed by realization of birthlessness.

You're crazed by practice of pacification.
I'm crazed by mahāmudrā experience.

This song of lunatics meeting
Is the empty echo of mahāmudrā.

Then Dampa revealed his true body and said, "You sing all the secret
Dharma and precepts in songs! You preach profound Dharma in the mar-
ketplace! What's more, your behavior is random and senseless! What will
you do when the ḍākinīs pass their judgment?"
So Mila sang:

To lama, personal deity, and ḍākinīs
I pray—grant me blessings.

In the great lion of boundless mind
The three fearless skills are complete,
And he sleeps in snow without melting the ice.
Let death come to this holder of vision—

When I die, I'll rejoice in death;
When death comes, I'll blissfully die.

My mind's a vulture without hope or fear
Who spreads his wings of method and wisdom united
And sleeps on the rock of natural reality.
Let death come to this meditator—
When I die, I'll rejoice in death;
When death comes, I'll arrive at bliss.

I'm a young tiger free from acceptance or rejection,
Smiling the smile of nonactivity,
Asleep at ease in the forest of gnosis.
Let death come to this practitioner—
When I die, I'll rejoice in death;
When death comes, I'll arrive at bliss.

I'm the little fish of natural-state awareness
Swimming the depths of reality's ocean,
Abiding in dharma-body's changeless state.
Let death come to this possessor of results—
When I die, I'll rejoice in death;
When death comes, I'll arrive at bliss.

At my right warriors stand like lions,
To my left heroines dance.
Dharma protectors wait before me like servants,
And practitioners follow me like dogs.

The Lineage of Word[18] arches above like a roof,
And below it ḍākinīs hover like a cloud.
Such a yogi-repa
Doesn't fear the passing of judgment.

Dampa thought to himself, "He does indeed have great confidence of view—but what about his powers?" So to test him Dampa Sangye multiplied himself into identical emanations seated on every pellet of animal dung. But Jetsün also multiplied himself into a Milarepa on the tip of every stalk of grass. In amazement Dampa said, "Your powers are exactly as you stated in your song! Now that we two siddhas—of India and of Tibet—have met, we should celebrate our association with a feast. Will you draw water or make a fire?"

Jetsün replied, "I'll draw the water." He went to a spring and scooped blue water the consistency of jelly into a net bag. On his return Dampa said, "This isn't enough water even for us two siddhas. We must offer the first portion of the feast to the warriors and ḍākinīs and the rest to all the masters and traders gathered here."

Mila replied, "Just light the fire."

So Dampa ignited a fire in the pile of rocks at the top of the pass. Jetsün said, "We'll need a pot." Dampa produced a skullbowl from his armpit, and when he placed it on the fire, it expanded to an enormous size. Jetsün drew water from the air and filled the skullbowl. He then stirred it and without adding anything it became full of a variety of foods. Placing it in front of Dampa, he offered the first portions of the feast to the ḍākinīs and divided the rest equally among the masters and traders. There was one piece left over. Jetsün said, "To whom should I offer this?" From the sky the ḍākinīs replied:

> Triple Gem and Dharma protectors are pleased by your service,
> Mother and ḍākinīs are satisfied by your feast,
> Dampa Sangye's content with your offering,
> Those gathered here have received their share—
> Take it yourself, yogi-repa.

Having sung this, the host of ḍākinīs prepared marvelous offerings and turned the wheel of the feast. They performed vajra-songs and music, and flowers rained from the sky. All present were amazed and received very great blessings. At the conclusion of this circle-feast all minds merged in profound communication. They discussed much Dharma, after which Jetsün sang:

> I bow to the feet of my skillful lama.
>
> This Indian Dampa Sangye
> Came to Thongla, Nyanang, in Tibet.
> Yogi Mila also came
> To see the face of this great being.
> We displayed the range of our miraculous powers

And turned the wheel of miraculous feast.
We were worshipped variously by ḍākinīs—
A rain of flowers fell from sky
And the sound of sweet music resounded.

We made much Dharma conversation,
Our minds merged in reality's depths.
All of you here were bestowed with fortune.

A fledgling eagle of fundamental consciousness,
I spread my wings of method and wisdom united
And flew into the sky-realm of reality.
With inquiring eye I looked in all directions—
I saw the abyss of three lower realms
And the fading sun-moon glow of high realms.

I saw massing clouds of good and bad action
And the rising, setting sun and moon of birth and death.
I saw the sky of actual-state reality.
I saw the superficial world as illusory dream.
I saw the inexpressible, unthinkable absolute.

Eh ma! Phenomena of superficial samsara
Don't exist—yet appear! Great wonder!

Dampa said, "My own Dharma lineage is like a fire—once lit it will burn out. Yours is like a river stream—it will flow a long way. Now I don't need you and you don't need me."

At this they both flew into the sky, going their separate ways like vultures scattering from a corpse.

Mila with the horned staff

10

Song of the Horned Staff

JETSÜN AND SEBEN REPA WENT TOGETHER to Upper Nyang in the province of Tsang. Traveling through unfamiliar territory, they reached the edge of a village where several men were gathered. Mila said to them, "We two yogis have a vow of begging only at the 'first door.' Someone who has strong faith give us some food."

A young man, in his thirties, asked, "Where are you from?"

"We've come to Tsang from Upper Tibet."

"It's said that a good yogi should be able to draw examples from any object or event. Sing us a song about the symbolic meanings of that antelope-horn staff in your hand; then I'll offer you food."

So Jetsün sang this song:

> I pray at the feet of Marpa, best of men,
> Who nurtured me with unstinting compassion
> While absorbed in the clear light of mahāmudrā
> In the dharma-body palace void and free of fabrication.
> Bless all beings to direct them to Dharma!
>
> Listen to this, patron-interrogator:
> This horn with spear shaft and rope windings
> That I the yogi hold in hand—
> Where is it from?
> It's from the northern land of the gods of wealth.
> Its origin in the land of the gods of wealth
> Symbolizes my wealth through knowing what's sufficient.
>
> It grew on an antelope's head.
> Its growth on a living being's head
> Symbolizes superficial reality.
>
> The horn itself is insentient, lifeless.
> This insentience and lack of perceiver
> Symbolizes absolute reality.

Cutting it from the animal's head
Symbolizes separation of body and mind;
Its massive root
Symbolizes knowledge of samsara's hidden root,
And its many ridges
Symbolize the overwhelming waves of misery
On samsara's great ocean.

This horn's three bends
Symbolize straying into the three lower states
Through evils produced by the three poisons;
The straight sections between the bends
Indicate that though we're now wandering in samsara,
The ultimate goal will at last be attained.

This horn's hollow inside
Symbolizes the hollowness of samsara;
Its dark color,
The changelessness of reality;
And its toughness and hardness,
The strong diligence in Dharma
Of me, the Tibetan yogi-repa.

This spear shaft below the horn
Indicates that I, Tibetan yogi-repa,
Fly like a shot arrow
Through the space of samsara's six realms.

The ten turns of rope at its base
Indicate that I, Tibetan yogi-repa,
Have arrived at the palace of dharma-body
By traveling the ten bodhisattva stages.

Sticking the horn's tip in the earth
Symbolizes the leading of hell beings dwelling below.
Or sometimes I lay it on the ground
To indicate the leading of frustrated spirits and animals.

Sometimes I point it at the sky
To symbolize the taming of gods and anti-gods,
And when I take it up and wander the countryside,
It symbolizes the taming and leading of humankind.

This handle hole bored through the staff
Shows how my mind penetrates appearances without obstruction;
This grip of soft buckskin
Indicates the yogi's suppleness of mind.
This tough, unbreakable thong handle
Indicates that I, Tibetan yogi-repa,
Have no fear of falling into lower states.

This song expresses the actual meaning,
But there's no assurance the symbols will be understood;
So now receive a song of explanation:

Carrying this horned spear
Symbolizes my battle with the dogs of hatred
While wandering the countryside aimlessly.

This short song from my lips
Indicates I seek sustenance by begging;
And the symbolic language of this song
Shows a yogi's childish prattling.

Understand its significance, gods and men!
Make it an inspiration to virtue!
Take it as a reminder for the faithful!

All the men were overwhelmed and asked Mila for blessings, saying, "Now we've met face to face the Milarepa of whom we've heard." They made offerings and requested Dharma instruction, but Mila fasted there for three days and then left.

MILA'S DYNAMIC PERSONALITY and active life exemplify the fact that the achievement of enlightenment is not the sort of "emotional death" imagined by some people. Buddhahood is not attained merely by suppressing the emotions; in fact, the tantric vehicle utilizes such usually disturbing elements as the very fuel of practice. The misconception of what personal development means has occurred at all times, so Mila explains what the attainment of buddhahood actually is. He rejects the ideas that infants and animals are naturally enlightened, that supernormal powers are an indication of realization, and that the practice of the blissful absorption levels leads in the direction of liberation. He then epitomizes the course of the path to enlightenment and closes with a long series of precepts.

11

Elimination of Desires

ONE DAY WHILE JETSÜN WAS STAYING in Medicine Valley of Chu Bar teaching Dharma to several disciples, the Yogi Ortön Gendün approached him and asked, "Precious lama, in the teachings of several geshes you are renowned as a buddha. They say you've totally eliminated desire. Is this true?"

Jetsün replied, "So they say. But there are many ways of eliminating desires. None of them are certain to yield buddhahood. You can understand the meaning of the term "buddha" by listening to this old man's song."

> I bow to the feet of great Marpa,
> Lotsawa who spoke two tongues,
> Who with vision of the three times
> Realized the reality of the many as one.

> Specifically, one who's cleansed and totally removed
> The mass of negative preconceptions and imprints
> And the obscurations of affliction and action
> Produced by the power of ignorance;
> Who's cleared the dark deluded aberration
> Obscuring knowledge of the objective world
> And obtained strengths, confidences, and unique properties[19]
> Through gnostic realization of the natural state—
> To such a one who's developed
> All the qualities of total omniscience
> The term "buddha" is applied.

> Such a perfect buddha
> Is perfectly free from all desires.

> To say that even bugs in trees
> And infants lacking clear conception
> Are buddhas is the talk of fools.
> Though lacking sophisticated concepts
> Like possessions and friends,

They're still tormented by reactions
To heat and cold, hunger and thirst.
These root associations gradually develop
Into full-blown concepts of desire.

Outsiders, sages, and the heterodox
Have numerous attainments
Like soaring flight through the sky,
Unobstructed clairvoyant knowledge,
Various magical transformations,
And freedom from cravings for the objects of desire.
But they'll revolve in samsara again and again
Through the fault of incorrect refuge-source
And lack of the vision
Of analytic wisdom and skill in methods.

Likewise, with Buddhist meditators—
Though they've traveled the four absorptions
And four formless media
To samsara's peak where desire is gone[20]—
If they're not imbued with wisdom and method,
They'll revolve in samsara as before.

Therefore, buddhahood will never be won
By merely stopping desires without integration
Of method and wisdom through skill in method.

So how is it done?
Study the paths of the three personality types:[21]
The six transcendences of giving and so on,
The four social means and four infinitudes,
The three vehicles and three bases of practice,
And the integration of compassion and voidness.

Then strive to compile a great store of merit
By transcendence of giving, morality, and patience.
Build up the store of gnosis
By practicing the transcendences of absorption and wisdom.
Vigor assists both

By intensifying mental effort.

Though everything is actually void,
Insistence on mere nominal "voidness"
Without actual voidness realization
Leads to denial of action and result,
The great cause of hell and loss of freedom.
Therefore, of good and bad actions and results
Avoid the sinful in the slightest degree,
And cultivate virtue to its greatest extent.

Strive also to cultivate inseparable union
Of both wisdom and absorption,
For by absorption the mind is stabilized,
And by wisdom strayings are detected.

Likewise, with voidness and compassion,
Cultivate the integration of wisdom and method,
For by that sublime method of great compassion
The welfare of beings in samsara is achieved,
And by wisdom's view of voidness
Dharma-body for one's own sake is realized.
From planted seed of supplication
Imbued with the sublime method of compassion
The resultant twofold form-body arises.
And by form-body's inconceivable emanations
The hopes, wants, and needs of beings
Are fulfilled in ways concordant with their welfare,
Like a gem that grants all wishes,
Or a wish-granting tree, or a divine tree of worship.

And omniscience also, free from preconception,
Fulfills the hopes of all trainees
As inconceivable, streaming rays of sun
Dissolve the fog of all the world.

The stages of such cultivation
Overflowing the mind of Marpa,
That king of all translators,

Are the range of Mila's realization.
I've explained to you, son Ortün,
This beggar-yogi's understanding—
Bear it in heart, O nobly born.

Till the natural state's been confronted
Through union of Dharma and your essential mind,
Don't disregard cause and effect.

Till you're free from fears of birth and death
By realizing appearances lack true reality,
Don't make empty, senseless talk.

Till you've attained skill
In all sūtras, tantras, and śāstras,
Don't teach Dharma pointlessly.

Till body, speech, and mind toward others' welfare are directed
By slashing entanglement with your own desires,
Don't behave with pretension and deceit.

Till you've slashed entanglement with your own desires
And can sacrifice life to benefit others,
Don't say, "I'm a bodhisattva."

Till engaged in others' welfare with four social means
Through inception of four infinitudes in mind,
Don't say, "I work for others' welfare."

Till your heart is one with your lama
And you pray to him four sessions each day,
Don't say, "I have admiration and respect."

Till beings and world shine as divine, without attachment,
And illusory-body's purified into clear light,
Don't say, "I'm a practitioner of the mantra vehicle."

Till ḍākinīs gather at your feast

And holy offerings change to nectar
Don't say, "I perform religious feasts."

Till mastery of white element, currents, and channels,
And the element can be emitted or held,
Don't perform karmamudrā.

Till the force of clear awareness rises
In brilliant, thought-free quiescence,
Don't say, "I meditate the absorptions."

Till essential reality is borne on brow
Through examination by analytic, gnostic wisdom,
Don't say, "Realization has dawned."

Do you understand my meaning, yogi?

Moved by strong faith, the yogi sang:

Eh ma! Great yogi-repa!
Eh ma! Protector of the three realms' beings!
Eh ma! Buddha with human form!
I bow to your feet, great Jetsün father.

Clouds of love and compassion
Gather in the infinite sky of your mind,
And with the resonant thunder of your speech
A rain of explicit Dharma falls.

You planted the seed of profound precepts
In the hard, untilled soil of my mind,
Irrigated with clear revelations,
Warded off the ruinous hail of mistaken thought,
And cultivated with timely, compassionate skill in method.

Though omniscient fruit hasn't ripened yet
By fault of my own inferior nature,
No one surpasses you in method.

From now till enlightenment's attained
May I accompany you, lord of yogis,
Inseparable always like body and shadow.

In your company may I realize the essence
Of natural state, and win enlightenment unexcelled.
May I then work for others' welfare
And thereby liberate all beings.

MILAREPA'S ATTITUDE TOWARD WOMEN often seems unnecessarily harsh. He frequently bore the brunt of their derision and laughter, especially when he arrived half-naked and unkempt at a party, as he does here. He responded with painfully direct criticism, but actually such rough treatment was given as a test, for he would take on as students only those who were able to recognize the cultural conditionings that defined their roles in society and who were willing to end them. This was true in his treatment of men as well as women, and once a woman understood the intent of his criticism—which was actually social, not sexual—she could become a fully qualified member of his following. A number of such women became accomplished yoginīs under his guidance.

12

Mila Gains a Young Woman Disciple at a Village Feast

ONCE THE GREAT JETSÜN MILAREPA was traveling in the Yardrog region begging food. He went up the street of a village named Bay Nyön and came to a house where many women were going in and out. He sat down just outside the door. A man arrived and said to him, "Inside we're drinking beer. Won't you join us, yogi?"

Mila replied, "I'd be glad to, but won't they complain?"

"They've no reason to say anything." The man shut his dog up, announced himself, and entered.

The crowd had gathered for a feast celebrating the birth of a son to a rich woman. The man called from inside, "Hey yogi in the doorway, I invited you in! Come get your share!"

Many women were present, talking and chattering. Some made comments like: "Hey yogi, have you ever had a wife?" "Who stole your clothes?" "We got our money's worth today—we've seen two skin shows." "There's a shameless yogi! If you know how to dress, I'll give you an old pair of pants."

They jibed and teased him thus, until the twenty-year-old daughter of the householder offered him a barley cake and a piece of meat with a skull-cap full of beer. She had the feeling that this yogi was one of the very best and said to him, "Great yogi, these women are burdened by inferior merit. The beer has gone to their heads, and they're just collecting a bunch of bad karma. Won't you sing a song about the faults of such women?"

Mila replied, "I don't know anything about it."

But the girl persisted, "I can tell by your scanty mode of dress that you must be highly practiced in meditation. With such open, candid behavior you must have realized the essential emptiness of the illusory world. With such forbearance and patience at this abuse, you must have the patience to practice Dharma. With such a radiant glow shining through the green reed-like color of your body, unafflicted by imbalances of the four elements of three vital principles,[22] you are certainly a realized practitioner of the difficult Dharma. With bare feet unscarred by rough gravel and thorns and unharmed by cold wind and ice, you must have obtained mastery over currents and channels. Your dynamic mind, your long, supple tongue beautiful as a lotus petal, and your broad, high throat indicate that you must embody a treasury of vajra song. Moreover, you are a great benefactor. All this must for the most part be so. Why won't you sing a song?"

At this the young woman's father interjected, "I'd hoped my daughter would be better than this! You're not much of a benefactress yourself. Don't ask him to sing for us crude folk—let him rest."

Her mother added, "I see just an ordinary beggar, and one who can barely talk, at that! Only you would heap praise on such a person. If you're so impressed, go follow him!" Saying this, she threw a handful of dirt at her.

The others joined in the derision and laughter. Jetsün thought, "If I don't sing, this young woman will also think I'm an idiot, and the others will gain much bad karma thereby. And any yogis who come begging after this will get a poor reception." So he suddenly sat up, holding his right hand to his cheek and planting the bone tip of his long staff in the ground with his left, and sang this song:

> Listen to this, "faithful patrons,"
> Usually scornful as gods,
> And abusive to me in particular—
> Listen, you ladies young and old:
>
> I was born from the seed of my unique father-lama,
> Constantly nurtured by mother wisdom-vision.
> I nursed at the breast of observance of cause and effect
> And was constantly warmed by the heat of profound precepts.
>
> I ate again and again the food of concentration
> And drank the draught of enlightenment mind.
> I wore the fine bliss warmth clothes of *tummo*
> Bound with the sash of precise recollective awareness.
>
> I wore boots of uplifting view on my feet
> Tied with the bootstrap of penetrating wisdom,
> Draped my shoulders with the deerskin of reflective humility,
> And wore the lambskin of patient resignation behind.
>
> I tied the mirror of clear introspection at my side
> And adorned my body with the fine ornament of morality,
> Posture relaxed in steady quiescence,

Mouth and body controlled by conscience and shame.[23]

My intellect is brilliant with alert memory,
Face is transfigured with introspective insight,
And broad intellect encompasses the five sciences.[24]

The pretty clear-light lady of method-wisdom union
Is enough of a wife for giving help to beings;
The spontaneous dharma-body is enough religion.

Thus all present in this full house,
Especially you "noble ladies" young and old,
And in particular you chattering women,
Still your noise and hear this song:

There's no possibility I'd be unable
To withstand your nonsense—
It's just your own disposition.
Bear this in mind, insignificant ones:

Attachment to your body, that heap of flesh and blood,
Is natural.
Your body's driven by bad mental conditionings, propensities,
And blown about by ephemeral winds.

When you're uncontrollably stirred up,
It's like a field of pigs and foxes in summer.
Don't keep watching this wanderer,
Twisting your head over your shoulders
Like goats intoxicated by clover.
Your eyes will dart anywhere, uncontrollably,
Like squinting into blinding sunlight
To see a handsome man.

Your mouths chatter senselessly
Like a necromancer possessed by a spirit.
Your minds and bodies flip about
Like the bodies of landed fish.
All streets are filled with your noise,

All roads of the land with your comings and goings.
You hang the wool basket from your head with a strap
And hold the spindle like a spear.

When you sew scraps together, it's a bag for stealing.
And if your neighbor complains about it you argue—
If you had the chance you'd steal your mothers' underpants!

If you see something nice, your monkey face smiles like the
    mouth of a bell;
If you don't like it, your face is like an angry camel.
While doing menial housework,
You hold baby on your lap like an unpaid debt.

While grinding three bushels of barley,
You eat one bushel yourself,
Spill half a bushel on the ground,
And are so proud of the few handfuls remaining.

You talk with mouth stuffed full of food,
Work the fire bellows with your knee,
Sit right down on the flour sacks,
And spill oil all over the stove.

You cast glaring looks at your husband
And are fierce as a tiger with your in-laws.
Your inbred children sit round the fire,
And you continually beat them with the poker.

Your calves should be firm but sag down;
Hair should hang down, but sticks up,
Poor diet has ruined your complexion,
And your lack of good clothing is disgraceful.

You work sorcery day and night to harass foes.
In the presence of such a zombie
Your stove becomes buried in a heap of ash
Accumulated over months and years
From burning reeds as in a time of famine.

Rotten, selfish women!
When you die, you'll go to preta country!

If I criticize, I'll criticize that;
You're not even impressed or cautious
With me the yogi, the self-risen vajra.

Listen yet more, fine ladies;
I'll describe a woman who's a queen of support:

Her hands and posture are relaxed and calm,
Mouth and body well controlled.
Intelligent and skilled in crafts,
She acts carefully through critical, recollective awareness.

She's cleanly, respectful, and determined,
Worships the Triple Gem as the highest,
And gives help to lowly impoverished persons.

She treats her family like something precious,
Is respectful of the old,
Protects servants like her own children,
And treats everyone according to their merits.

She knows how to collect the merit of giving
And keeps vows of abstinence[25] at the proper time.
She practices layman's Dharma with enthusiasm,
And when a practice is suitable, she takes it up.

May all who've had pleasant
Or unpleasant contact with me
Share in enlightenment.

Everyone joyfully concurred and became inspired about Dharma. The young woman's father said, "My daughter is smart after all! You are exactly as she said." He paid respects to Jetsün and requested Dharma association with him.

The young woman then asked if she could practice Dharma. Her mother replied, "It's true she always did say she wanted to practice Dharma. But there's still a problem. She was promised in marriage to the worthy son of a wealthy man just yesterday. You ought to do what's proper."

But her father countered, "This daughter of mine is intelligent. It's fitting for her to practice Dharma. Don't stop her—the bad results of preventing Dharma practice are very great. If you wish to practice Dharma, I'll have your younger sister fulfill the agreement. That's good enough. Do what you wish to do."

At this many of the other women urged her, "Go ahead, practice Dharma."

She begged Jetsün. Seeing that she was determined, he gave her Dharma instruction and empowerments. She practiced at Semodo and later became a great siddha, after which she aided many beings. The great Jetsün was very pleased.

An angry old woman shouts at Milarepa

13

Mila Resurrects an Old Woman

THEN THE GREAT JETSÜN RETURNED to White Rock Horse Tooth Cave and instructed the young repas, headed by Seben Repa, in *tummo* yoga. He told them, "All of you devote yourselves to practice." He then went with Rechung Dorje Drakpa up to the great Pelmo plateau to beg.

Arriving at Ber Tser on the Pelmo plateau, they went to beg at a large encampment. An old woman shouted, "Yogis! Spoilers! Killers! Are you planning to trick and rob me? Are you thinking I'm unable to manage my wealth, cattle, horses, and sheep? Those tents to the right belong to my sons and grandsons. Those to the left are the tents of my sons-in-law. Best not come around here!"

So Jetsün sang her this song:

> I pray to the holy guardian of beings—
> Protect me with unwavering attention.
>
> Hair turned white, but oblivious to Dharma,
> Face full of wrinkles, but heedless of death,
> Eyes sunk in flesh, but glaring in anger,
> Mouth toothless, but still uttering curses,
> Body bent, but trying to be sexy.
> Listen here, wealthy lady,
> Selfish and full of pride:
>
> You're riding the horse of intense desire,
> Holding in hand the spear of hatred,
> With the black band of delusion tied round your head.
>
> Driven by the whip of jealous envy,
> You fill the countryside with your proud yelling.
> You bear the weight of stinginess on your back
> And hoist high your load of sins.

You surround yourself with the ten evils
And turn your back on the Triple Gem.
You've thrown out the ten good virtues
And have continual enmity for holy Dharma.

Carrying this wealth of ripened sins,
You'll take some rest in the animal realm,
Stop a while in the land of pretas,
And make your home in the realms of hell.

The misery of animal stupidity is the least;
Worse yet is that of hunger and thirst,
And worst is the pain of hellish torture.

O woman who seeks to gain advantage,
When these troubles fall on your head,
Don't make too loud a lament!

In extreme rage she yelled, "Yogi, if you have such vicious criticism for people, why come around begging?" And pulling out a side pole of her tent she hit Jetsün many times.

Jetsün said, "Oh Rechungpa, when afflictive emotions arise, apply the antidote. Meditate patience." And he sang this song:

I pray to my compassionate lama.

I've produced the mind aimed at supreme enlightenment;
And realizing all beings are my parents,
I return their harmfulness with help—
How could I ever have an angry feeling?

Old woman enmeshed in bad actions,
May this harm you've done me
Be a source of help to you
In all your future lives.

The complete series of empowerments I've received
Transform apparent world into deity's body,
Lead me to hear all sounds as mantra,

And illumine thought forms as dharma-body—
How could I ever be angry with you?

All things are naturally like space.
Space itself has no characteristics—
It neither exists by nature,
Nor is it nonexistent—
It transcends dualistic thought.

I, the space-like yogi,
Have seen the nature of space.

Lying down at the edge of a sandy expanse of ground, he slept. As he got up early the next morning, he heard sounds of weeping. A short while later a man came, and after paying respects, said, "Precious lama, that old woman, my mother, died last night. Would you come help conduct the funeral?"

Rechungpa said, "It must have been the ḍākinīs' condemnation of that old woman."

So teacher and disciple went, and after blessing the corpse, Mila sang:

Homage to my father lamas—
Bless us to be mindful of impermanence and death.

Looking back on the land of my birth,
Impermanent place like a city of spirits,
It appeared a city, but was nothing—thus I was sad;
But on considering it my mind became happy.
Don't consider homeland permanent, fortunate ones.

Looking back on the friends I've had,
Impermanent circle like the inn at a market
Where travelers gather at night and leave at morning,
They appeared an unbroken circle, but scattered—thus I was sad.
Don't consider friends permanent, fortunate ones.

Looking back on the possessions I gathered
Impermanent wealth like a honeybee's honey,
Gathered by me, but enjoyed by others—thus I was sad.
Don't consider wealth permanent, fortunate ones.

Looking back on the apparent world,
Impermanent appearances like a rainbow in sky,
Like a rainbow dissolve—thus I was sad.
Don't consider appearances permanent, fortunate ones.

Looking back on the flow of my breath,
Impermanent breath like morning mist,
As mist condenses and dissolves—thus I was sad.
Don't consider breath permanent, fortunate ones.

Looking back on my mind's self-awareness,
Impermanent awareness like a fledgling on treetop,
That can't maintain its perch—thus I was sad.
Don't consider mind permanent, fortunate ones.

Looking back on this body of my birth,
Impermanent body like the old woman's last night,
And like that old woman it will die—thus I was sad;
But on considering it my mind became happy.
Don't consider body permanent, fortunate ones.

All those present were affected and offered their services. They said, "The old woman unwittingly abused a buddha who came to her door. She brought this punishment on herself."

They carried the body to the edge of the plateau. Jetsün sat in concentration and drew her consciousness-principle back into her body.

Then he taught them about death with this song:

Homage to the vajra-body—
Consciousness purified in the state of gnosis,
Perfected in the clear light of reality
Emanating bodies to provide impartial help for beings.

With the iron hook of deep concentration
I drew the disembodied consciousness
Of this old woman
Back from its wanderings in bardo existence.

With the mahāmudrā's great seal of gnosis
I've now sealed it into her body,
And by repetition of profound mantras
Cleansed its obstructions and propensities for sinful action.

Let this be an inspiration to you;
Listen in confidence to my song:

The changing of life is called death:
Complexion changes; face becomes pale;
Nose, dry and cracked; teeth, coated.
Eyes bulging from sockets
Stare in terror at others' faces.

When the end is near, breath comes
In short gasps rattling in throat.
One knows all will be left behind—
Hoarded possessions and loving friends.

Still unwilling—it's time to go.
Nothing will follow
Save one's virtue and sin.
Consumed thus with sorrow
Death agonies are felt.

In this life it's experienced once,
But this one-time experience
Isn't the end of it—
In future lives it will be the same,
Like the turning of a water wheel.
To break this cycle,
Attain the dharma-body state.
Focused thus in natural reality
The miseries of ignorance
Are ended, confusion gone.

They stood there wide-eyed as a rainbow radiated from the woman's body. Jetsün sang again:

I pray to my father lamas.

This selfish old woman
Wandering the bardo leading to birth
Was physically transformed to deity's clear-light body
By production stage of profound mantra vehicle
Through the efforts of Milarepa himself.

Her sin-laden consciousness was drawn
By the iron hook of mudra concentration,
Its obstructive taint of sin instantly cleansed
By the flowing stream of mantra recitation.

She was set face to face with mind's actual state
By the essence of the profound path of method,[26]
And carried to the dharma-body palace
On the steed of mahāmudrā.

May I provide spontaneous help to beings
Till samsara's end.

All present were overwhelmed and sought Dharma association, empowerment, and blessings. They made many offerings, but Mila rejected them, singing:

In possession of the wealth of satisfaction
I find worldly possessions much trouble.
I don't want them—take them yourselves.

However, through the merit of dedicating them to me
The afflictional and objective obscurations
Will be purged from your minds.

And after you've entered the middle path
To freedom from fabrication of the four extremes,[27]
Through completion of the stores of merit and gnosis,
May you arrive at omniscient gnosis.

In the state of reality all things—
Virtuous and sinful—are illusion.
In the self-aware clear light of the dharma-body
Everything's totally dissolved in nonduality.

Jetsün stayed there several days, and all the people were fulfilled by their Dharma association with him.

THE GROUP OF PIECES entitled "Six Vajra Songs" chronicles the events of a long journey undertaken by Milarepa and Rechungpa. It provides further examples of Mila's encounters and behavior with the common people of Tibet. It forms an independent subcollection in the *Stories and Songs from the Oral Tradition of Jetsün Milarepa* prefaced with this statement by the patron who had them transcribed and printed:

> Although the "Six Vajra Songs" are very holy and secret, Lhe Tsünpa Rinchen Namgyel had them printed at this late date solely with the intention of helping others. May the lamas and host of ḍākinīs forgive me.

14

From the "Six Vajra Songs"

ONCE JETSÜN AND RECHUNGPA were making a long journey together. Traveling north of the Tsangpo river, they came to a place called So. There were many herdsmen; so they went to beg. One man told them, "Begging food each day is a problem. I'll give you a bag so you can collect food from everyone here. You don't even have suitable clothing to stay here awhile."

So Jetsün sang him this song:

> Precious, peerless savior of beings
> Come to dwell at the crowns of our heads,
> And guiding us with unwavering attention
> Let blessings for siddhis fall like rain.
>
> Faithful patrons,
> By your gift of carrying bag
> And considerate advice
> May your stores be completed
> And obscurations cleansed.
>
> There's but little breath left
> On the boundary of this life and next.
> Not knowing if I'll be here next morning,
> Why try to trick death
> With life schemes for a permanent future?
>
> I eat whatever food I get;
> Take my nourishment as ascetics do.
> I've done it all this human life,
> And I'll now continue my usual way.
> I don't want the bag of patrons.

Struck with strong faith, the herdsman paid respects, saying, "I have no cotton robe that isn't ragged. Please accept this felt."

In reply Mila sang another song:

Driven by delusion-caused affliction and action,
This naked, insubstantial consciousness
Wanders the city of six illusory realms
And sleeps in the highways of birth, death, and bardo.

It's driven by waves of obsessive desire,
Burnt by the fires of intense aversion,
And wrapped in the dark cloud of delusion.

Toppling to the abyss from the pinnacle of pride,
Pelted by the cold wind of envy,
It sinks into the mire of samsaric cravings.

Climbing the rocky ledge of bardo and dream,
It falls into the abyss of affliction and instinct,
Swept away by the current of confused, evil action.

Burning with deluded ideas of the apparent,
It rests only in the darkness of unconsciousness.
Struggling through the abysmal bardo to birth
It's blown by strong karmic winds to the ten directions.

Its own four physical elements turn against it;
Earth element is saturated with water,
Space element totally consumed in fire.
The deep darkness of karma descends
As it sinks in the mire of intense, fearful sensations.

But from a lama possessing the power of blessing
Beg the profound instructions for the path
Which leads to the place of liberation
From the fearful events brought on by such action.

Reveal the true state of birth, death, and bardo!
Rip the sack of lies of bardo and dream!
Force out the true nature of the bardo of birth!
Turn all illusion inside out!
See the actual essence of mind.

Let realization of the natural state shine.
Throw out the attachment of egoism.
Release attachment which clings to things.

With bliss warmth of *tummo* ablaze in my body
This mere cotton robe is quite enough.
I eat the ready-made food of concentration,
Take in the essence of nettles and stones.[28]
Quench my thirst at the stream of enlightenment,
Even savor a bit of my own shit and piss.[29]

I rely on the constant wealth of contentment,
And sorrow for friends in the six realms of samsara.
Sometimes I go impartially begging,
Always wandering the wilderness aimlessly.

In winter I sleep in mountain retreats,
Cotton robe burning like a fire
Summer I sleep in torrid valleys,
Cotton robe cool as a breeze.

Springtime I rest on the gravel of canyons,
Cotton robe soft as wool.
In autumn I go out begging alms,
Cotton robe light as a feather.
Are you really happy, yogi?
Is there another as happy as me?

With this song he rejected the felt. Everyone was strongly impressed and requested Dharma association with him. That particular patron gave up all his affairs and followed after Jetsün, eventually becoming a yogi with a foothold on the path.

ဇာ ⚡ ဇာ

After crossing the Tsangpo river they traveled south, descending through the pastures and farmlands of Mar. At one village square a crowd was gathered, and Jetsün called out, "Anyone with faith—give this day's food to us two yogis!"

A youth replied, "I've seen beggars, but none more decrepit than you two! You don't have clothes to cover your bodies or a bag to carry food or even an attitude of humility. You don't need to beg from me—you've already provided me with a real show!"

A young woman prepared some barley meal and served it with butter and a bowl of yogurt, saying, "Now you can collect food from the others too."

Jetsün replied, "That's enough for today. We keep the vow of begging only at the 'first door.' Even if we collected food from the others, we have no container to hold it or bag to carry it."

The youth spoke up again, "You've got no song, no chant, no drum, no blessing, no prayer, no appreciation, no thanks, no clothes, and no shame."

Another man added, "If you know any song, sing it."

So Jetsün sang this song:

> Precious lama, guide to the true path,
> I pray to you—grant me blessings.
>
> Now listen, eloquent young man:
> By the kindness of my unique father-lama
> I was reared with paternal method and love,
> Nursed at the breast of maternal wisdom of voidness,
> And nourished on the food of profound integration.
>
> I've now perfected experience and skill,
> Introspective transformation into the divine,
> With powerful awareness of the natural state,
> Inner strength of vision, meditation, and practice,
> And bliss-warmth of *tummo*'s AH[30] aglow in body.
>
> Mounting the illusory horse of mind and currents,
> I gallop away from the Lord of Death
> And pass through the city of blissful liberation.
> Through the virtue of this woman's gift
> May all beings, led by her,
> Have long healthy life and happiness—
> And attain perfect buddhahood in the end.
> Young man, at the time of your death
> May you enter the clear light of the dharma-body

With consciousness and memory unclouded,
Experiencing the stages of death till clear-light dawns.

Everyone paid respects and circled him. The young man offered his apology, and in great faith the young woman asked for teaching, removing a turquoise from her neck as an offering. Jetsün rejected it with this song:

I pray to my lamas—
Grant your blessings to these faithful.

This precious gem of the clear light
Of gnosis primally pure
Was set in the clasp of compassion and voidness,
Polished with the clarity of introspection,
And strung on the thread of the natural state.

This is the birthstone of me, the yogi.
I don't want your jewelry;
But by the merit of offering it to me
With faith and devotion,
May you complete your stores of merit and gnosis
And have the fortune of the excellent form-body
Adorned with all auspicious signs.

May you have the fortune of long, healthy life.
May you have the fortune of happiness for now.
May you have the fortune of nirvana in the end.
May you have the fortune of dharma-body for your own sake,
And the form-body for the sake of others.

☙ ❧ ☙

Invited by the people, they remained a few days teaching the Dharma, after which they traveled for a day through Tra Rum. They stayed in an abandoned house that night and left early the next morning. On the way they met a woman carrying water. Mila caught hold of the hem of her robe and said, "Hey, give us yogis some breakfast!"

"Greedy yogis!" she replied, shaking the hem of her robe, "Where are you coming from—grabbing me and demanding that I provide for your belly?

You should take care of my stomach! I'm sure you have a place of your own—go farm it and eat. You have a human body just like me."

So Mila sang her this song about distinguishing the similar:

> The actual mind, clear and void,
> Has been likened to space—
> But comparison of mind with space won't hold,
> For mind is aware, though void,
> While space is voidness devoid of awareness.
> They're similar in their voidness,
> But very different in actuality.

> The actual mind, clear and void,
> Has been likened to the sun and moon—
> But comparison of mind with sun and moon won't hold,
> For mind is clear and unsubstantial;
> While sun and moon are clear but solid.
> They're similar in their clarity,
> But very different in actuality.

> This actual mind, clear and void,
> Has been likened to that mountain up there—
> But comparison of mind with mountain won't hold,
> For mind is uncompounded
> While that mountain's composed of atoms.
> They're similar in their unchangingness,
> But very different in actuality.

> This actual mind, clear and void,
> Has been likened to that river down there—
> But comparison of mind with river won't hold,
> For mind is uncompounded
> While that river's the conflux of many streams.
> They're similar in their constant flow,
> But very different in actuality.

> This actual mind, clear and void,
> Is said to be alike for me and you—

But comparison of me with you won't hold.
You're involved in mundane affairs:
Distracted with drudgery all day,
Stupefied with sleep at night,
A slave to desire dawn till dusk.

I'm an ascetic yogi:
I work for the welfare of beings all day,
I'm focused in clear light all night,
Worshipping with tormas from dawn till dusk.
We're similar in our human bodies,
But very different in the success of our lives.

The woman was extremely impressed and finally invited them into her house where she treated them with great respect. She had her hair cut, changed her name, and requested instruction for mahāmudrā practice, offering a nugget of gold for the initiation fee. Later she became a woman of excellent realization.

As a religion becomes established in the form of institutions, certain faults seem inevitable in any age. The relevance of Mila's comments in this story is striking. He has stopped at a large religious center of both laymen and monks. His bold behavior attracts the attention of a young man, and their subsequent interaction is a good example of Mila's subtle skill in changing the attitudes of the people he met. The youth is critical at first, impolitely offering Mila inferior food. He's impressed by Mila's first song, but still clings to his belief in formal religious structures. After Mila's second song criticizing false, pretentious religious leaders he tries to hedge, more impressed with Mila but still believing that the religious center is the best life for practitioners. Mila's next song concerns the faults of lax religious followers, complacent in their compliance with religious forms. The young man is left only with his faith in the head of his own center, so Mila discreetly advises him to be cautious in accepting a religious guide. Finally getting the point, he asks for Mila's definitive advice on the tantric lifestyle practiced and advocated by his teachers, to which Mila replies with a song clearly delineating the proper order and prerequisites of tantric practice. In correcting the most common misconceptions about tantric practice, he points out the danger of incorrect application of sensory gratification and negative elements in practice before the prerequisite generation of the mind-for-enlightenment.

15

Mila Visits a Religious Center

ONE SUMMER AFTER SPENDING the winter at Lachi, the great Jetsün went begging in Upper Tibet. Traveling upwards through the highlands of that region, he came to a large religious center. A crowd of people had gathered for a feast in honor of the newly appointed head of the center. Walking right in, he sat down in the ranks of monks and helped himself to some food. A young man said to him, "Yogi, you seem to be in as good a physical condition as anyone born into this world—not too old and not too young. Now, in the prime of your strength, you should earn your food by doing physical labor; you wouldn't have to beg your food. Why put up with such ragged clothes?"

Saying this he tossed Jetsün some grain with pickles and in return Mila sang him this song:

> Precious Dharma lord whose mere memory's enough
> Grant us blessings from your unmanifest state.
>
> High-class youth raised by a good father,
> Gutsy man nurtured by a kind mother—
> Your lineage is founded on accumulated merit
> And your current glory springs from previous charity.
>
> Possessed of knowledge through intelligence,
> Attractive with an array of ornaments,
> You're the mainstay of a loving family.
> With strength and courage you overcome enemies,
> And with broad disposition please your relations.
>
> Involved in Dharma through natural faith,
> Generous to religion through small attachment to wealth,
> You're devoted to Dharma from the depths of your mind.
> Of a youthful offspring such as this
> Even I would be fond.
> But before father you're fierce as a tiger;
> Before mother fierce as a leopard.

In front of your wife you rear up like a bear,
But faced with an enemy you flee like a fox.

Among friends you stand like a lion;
Facing beggars, you roar like thunder.
You view monks as your enemies,
And treat laymen like gods.

You work out of craving for beer.
Daytime you hunt deer and slaughter beasts,
Nighttime indulge in adultery and theft,
Your life is filled with empty promises.

Through all this thievery and adultery
In the company of like-minded peers
You'll someday lose to the hands of bandits
Or incur the displeasure of your countrymen.

Someday the body you hold so dear
Will be inflicted with all sorts of punishment
Through the laws of local government.
Thrown into an intolerable, dark dungeon,
You'll be deprived of your precious life, perhaps,
Or some blood—or an eye—
Or exiled with just the clothes on your back,
All wealth subject to confiscation.
Then, in your unbearable hunger,
Everyone will despise you as a beggar.

I'm a yogi who takes things as they come—
I've happiness both this life and next.
I'm just telling you this, young man,
For I much appreciate your offering.

The youth replied, "Your song hit it right on the head! You're a quick-witted, eloquent yogi. Still, aren't you being a bit extreme with your simple and strict ways? I'm afraid that even the solitary buddhas haven't said not to wear clothes for protection of one's body. Since work doesn't suit you, you should stay at some suitable religious center and be a guide for lay people through your great skill in Dharma—just like our own monastery head. I think you'd have a satisfying future in this life and the next. What do you think about that, yogi?"

In reply Mila sang this song:

I pray to the feet of my lama.

First, cut through the confusion of learning;
Then ponder the meaning of what was learned;
And lastly meditate its meaning as instructed.

Imbued with compassion and voidness
By skill in the three divisions of scripture[31]
And in the injunctions of the three commitments[32]
At the root of all the Buddha's teachings,
And motivated by love and compassion,
Gain skill in teaching and guiding others.
Maintain high vision in tending your interests,
Balancing the interests of yourself and others.

Then amassing virtue from the smallest on up,
Shunning evil from the smallest on down,
Carefully observing cause and effect,
And holding firm to the enlightened mind
Disregard your own welfare
And act for others in whatever you do.
A person who upholds Buddha's teachings like this
Will raise the hairs on one's body when seen or heard.

But initially motivated by eight worldly concerns,
Desiring fine things in this present life,
One raises one's self to the position of teacher
And takes the name Geshe Tönba.[33]

One learns to perform rituals for food and drink,
Working hard to amass material wealth.
Everyone's pleased—"What wonderful chanting!"—
So he's appointed head of a religious center.
Everyone bows and offers respect,

While smiling he receives the sons of nobility.
But he won't even see a hungry man
And though gracious when offered food and goods,
Without an offering he can't even be met.
He collects an entourage of monk imitations
And pretending to offer circle feasts
Entertains for days with food and drink,
Receiving praise for his "greatness of merit."

His whole life's wasted on this crooked path—
In dealing, usury, farming, and business
Conducted with legal tricks and deceit.

Such a crook and shyster completely involved
In all sorts of evil action
Is called the mainstay of the religious center!

Once ordained into Buddha's teachings,
One should abandon attachment to material things—
Just take things as they come—
And holding fast to the enlightenment mind
Tend to the welfare of other beings.

But after putting on the yellow robe,
They have more business affairs than laymen!
They make this opportunity of human life
Obtained just once in a hundred births
An anchor cast into the sea of samsara!
A broom to sweep away their own liberation!
A guide to lead them to lower states!
Though they regret it when dying, what can be done?

I've seen a lot of such stuff.
I've no interest in running a religious center.
Take this as the answer to your question.

The young man got up, and serving a pitcher of beer to Jetsün, told him, "What you say is true; being a lama is a very tricky business. If you devote yourself to practicing Dharma, the monastery affairs will be neglected, and if you're involved in monastic affairs, your Dharma practice will suffer. But your lack of clothes still bothers me. If you had some helpful support, your practice would benefit. You wouldn't be so exhausted in tending to your everyday needs. Please stay here at this monastery and take part in the practice and material support. If the barley meal and other necessities provided aren't sufficient, I'll supplement them myself. Others would also help support you. In particular, today I'll give you enough woolen cloth to make a robe. Please accept my offer."

But again Jetsün replied with a song:

I pray to the feet of my father lama.

Son—faithful patron—listen here;
Preserve pure morality for your own sake,
Have love and compassion for the sake of others.
Strive always to work for the welfare of both.

Treat with respect and follow the words
Of abbots, teachers, and elders.
Guide with Dharma those younger than you
And exercise impartiality and regard for peers.

Be versed in key injunctions of the three commitments
And preserve your vows like the pupil of your eye.
Be skilled in the essential elements of ritual
And make earnest practice your foremost concern
Without regard for wealth or fame.

Extremely rare is such harmonious
And devoted service to the teaching—
Difficult for anyone to achieve.

Here in Tibet Dharma practice
Is mostly pretension of righteousness;
Spouting the nine profound precepts from mouth,
With heart set only on silver and gold.

Jealousy of superiors, competition with peers,
Circle feasts given solely for gain,

Charity practiced solely for fame,
Big shows given with partiality,
And necessities provided for profitable returns—
Such things are going on
Among pretentious, self-righteous followers of Dharma.

Others who wear the yellow robe—
Short on faith and long on hatred,
With little patience and much desire—
Are distracted with material affairs all day,
Obsessed with food from dawn till dusk,
And sunk at night in the stupor of sleep.

Outside they wear the yellow robe,
But their houses are filled with ill-gotten goods,
Their egos untouched by the millstone of Dharma.

Not realizing their minds' true nature,
They pour talk of voidness from their mouths
And in company of drunkards proclaim the secrets
Of profound Mantra Vehicle Dharma.

Before the ranks of scholars
They sit like dumb pigeons,
But when teaching profound Dharma,
Dodge the issue with skill.

Their whole life's wasted on senseless talk.
When they see a woman, they have a smiling come-on,
And not contented with their own companions,
Run around to places frequented by women.

Minds as stiff as a dried-up tree,
Personalities more unmanageable than an overgrown field,
They have faith smaller than a sesame seed
And random interest flowing beyond the Tsang river.

If there's food they'll hang around,
But have excuses for dropping religious duties.

To one's face they'll praise and eulogize,
But behind one's back turn quickly to abuse.

Such vow-breaking Dharma companions
Are a cause for rebirth in vajra-hells.
Thus I'm a yogi wandering aimlessly,
Mind sporting in a land of bliss.

Your advice moved by unbearable concern
Was well intended and marvelous.
But in the beginning I came unclothed and naked
From within my mother's womb,
And when the forces of this life are spent,
My disembodied mind will go forth naked.
So I'll leave things as they are.
I don't want your offer.

Again the young man said, "Very true. I have more to ask, but I'll leave it for later. In epitomizing the teachings of the vehicles this lama has taught profound Dharma helpful in the next world, and especially good advice for this present life. To my mind—with regard to leaders in this present life—the head of this center seems to be all right. Could you explain some of his faults?"

So again Mila sang:

I pray to the feet of my father lama.

Treat with respect the community of practitioners
Who desire happiness for all
Through the foundation of enlightenment-mind,
For they are the yardstick for straightening the crooked
In regulating laws of society by Dharma.

Protect the desperate with compassion and love;
Be a leader of the respectable and good,
And a firm corrector of the low and evil.

Now in the time of this degenerate age
Such a truly incorrupt social system
Well regulated by good Dharma

Is very, very rare
Because of the collective poverty of beings' merits.

These days the rulers and teachers of Tibet
Have broken the golden yoke of social laws.
Leaderless, unruly, and fragmented,
The land is full of bandits and robbers
Who pass their lives in evil pursuits,
Assaulting and killing for just one meal.

Upholders of the ways of righteous people
Are weak as stars in the early dawn,
While the heads of evil, destructive folk
Are high as the stalks of wild grass,
And starving paupers and beggars
Proliferate like leaves in springtime.

Expansive, totally helpful minds
And people who act with the ten positive virtues
Are as scarce as stars in daytime,
While attitudes destructive to one's self and others
And people who act with vicious evil
Flourish like a fine crop of grain.

During such an age as this,
Don't have interest or attraction
For those acting as rulers and teachers of others.

Even the leaders of a golden age
Bearing the miserable sins of all
Must be reborn into lower states.
Therefore, patrons endowed with faith,
Don't discriminate against the lowly.

"Very true," he again agreed. "These tantric teachers say they have the great qualities to attain buddhahood in this lifetime, or during death or bardo, or after seven or sixteen lifetimes at most. They also say that the sensory pleasures of this life are the path itself—that it's all right to gather possessions, have lovers, produce children, and indulge in food and alcohol.

Is this true? If it's all right to do this, I'd rather do so. How is it?"
Mila again replied in song:

I bow to my lama's feet.

Son and patron, listen and be happy:
Generally speaking, if you wish to leave samsara
You must also abandon the eight worldly concerns.

If you wish to gain the freedom of nirvana,
You must stick to basic morality of the three commitments,
Practice the path of the six transcendences,
Carefully observe the cause and effect of action,
And develop purity of view.

Then you can realize appearances as deity's body,
Understand all sound as mantra,
Know all thought as dharma-body,
Clarify the deities of the production stage,
Stabilize the yoga of the completion stage,
Make currents and channels fit for action,
And incorporate sensory pleasures into the path.
This was taught for the benefit of trainees.

It's improper here and now
To give such profound and secret precepts.
In fact, if it's hard to keep mere novice's vows,
The profound commitments of the Mantra Vehicle
Are extremely difficult to keep.

Tantric teachers of current times
Are tantric yogis only in name.
If liberation's attained by taking a name,
You too, no doubt, could attain liberation
By calling yourself a buddha!

In particular, these tantric teachers living like laymen,
Accepted thus by yourself,
Are mostly concerned with this present life

Because of the power of afflictive emotions.

Drunk on intoxicating beer,
They beat their old drums senselessly,
And in front of those unfit to hear it
Spout out secret mantras like shamen—
Thus the seventh major lapse[34] falls on them like rain.

Since the supreme bliss of the enlightenment-mind
Must first be roused at the crown of one's head,
If you start out by stirring up the emotions,
You'll only run counter to tantric Dharma.[35]

If I speak too much of this kind of thing
It might only serve to anger others,
So right here and now I can't say much.

There's a common adage:
"There's no way to perform acrobatics
Without putting your back to the ground."
Likewise, without difficult practice
Buddhahood can never be won.
Keep this in mind, youthful patron.

He caught hold of Jetsün's feet and begged him, "Precious lama, you're a great being who's detached his mind from the things of this life. If you don't take care of me, everything you've said just now is pointless. If I fail to obtain the Dharma after meeting a great siddha, it would be better to die— no way out but to die right here!"

He refused to be dissuaded. Giving up his involvement with family, friends, and possessions, he followed his lama, and by persevering in practice later became the siddha named Repa Sangye Gyap.[36]

BÖN IS THE NATIVE RELIGION of Tibet. At the arrival of Buddhism it was basically a simple shamanism emphasizing healing, supernormal abilities, destructive powers, and so on. As Buddhism gained ground the two religions vied for the faith and patronage of the people, the interaction resulting in a gradual broadening of scope and assimilation of Buddhist ideas by the Bönpos. This process was well under way by Mila's time, as indicated in this story, but Mila is emphatic in delineating the validity and advantages of the Buddhist path.

16

Confrontation with a Bön Priest

ONCE THE GREAT BEING KNOWN AS JETSÜN MILAREPA was headed for Ti Se
snow mountain with five disciples to meditate. One disciple fell sick and
being unable to continue, they spent the summer meditating on a desolate
mountain in Upper Lowo.[37] Some people saw them and were curious:
"Who could live for any length of time on that barren mountain?"
Realizing it was yogi Milarepa, they offered their respects and asked for
teaching. Mila sang to them:

> Lowo is the devil's dark country.
> Towns are the devil's prisons.
> Respect and status are the devil's ropes.
> Distraction is the devil's obstruction.
>
> Here, in desolate mountains empty of men,
> Yogic awareness blossoms.
> Here focused concentration grows strong.
>
> Rest you well, you gathered here—
> I supplicate for your fortune and spiritual welfare.

Saying this, he started to go. They called after him, but he didn't listen.
"Harvest time is here. You all have work to do. I'm going to look for winter
provisions." As he departed the men and women patrons and their children
accompanied him to the top of the Kora Pass. There they bowed, circled
him, and fervently asked him to stay. Finally they said, "We may not meet
you again, great Jetsün. Grant us protection now, in the bardo, and in
future lives."

The events of that occasion and the songs Mila sang are recorded in the
great *Hundred Thousand Songs*.[38]

Mila's disciples had also accompanied him to the Kora Pass and then
returned to Lowo to beg. Meanwhile, Jetsün continued on to Ti Se with
Seben Repa. On the central plateau of Drosho many herdsmen had gathered
and Mila and Seben went to beg. In front of a large tent was a man who

appeared to be a Bönpo priest receiving the offerings of the herdsmen. They approached and sat down. The leftovers from the offerings to the local Bönpo were collected and given to them.

Mila and Seben remained seated throughout the Bönpo's service, but when he was about to give the closing dedication, they got up to leave. The priest asked them angrily, "Why won't you listen to my dedication?"

"My dedication is different from yours. We should say them separately."

"Well, say yours."

"It's not necessary for you to listen to my dedication."

"Well, then, it's not necessary for you to concern yourself with a dedication on behalf of this tail and breast of yak given to me."

"I also have the right to make a dedication for this skin left over from the offerings made to you."

The priest was exasperated, "I won't take my hat off for your dedication, but you can pray for your leftover skin—I'll listen to what you say."

So Mila sang:

> Consistently kind lama,
> Personal deity who grants siddhis,
> Triple Gem worthy of everyone's respect,
> Oceanic multitude of guardians of teaching—
> Pray keep me always in mind.

> By the virtuous merit
> Of giving leftover food
> To yogis begging for alms,
> May all beings, headed by
> You patrons and your children,
> Obtain the best happiness in this life.

> May you lack suffering at the time of death,
> Take a divine or human body of leisure and opportunity
> In all situations of rebirth,
> And after enjoying the best of lives
> Obtain omniscience in the end.

> May all alms-seeking yogis,
> Multitude of spirits, and so on,
> Satisfied by this leftover offering

Attain the pure realm of reality.

In truth, this offering, dedication, and donors,
Requestor of dedication, dedicator, and so on
Are like a dream, illusion, and echo,
Like a mirage and flowers in the sky.

The Bönpo lama then said, "This is an example of the saying: 'Out of the trash heap a tiger emerges.' Who are you? Where are you from? What is your lineage? Where did you study? What is your practice?"

In reply, Mila sang this song:

I bow to the feet of my lama
Who transforms earth into gold,
Gold into wish-fulfilling gem,
And wishing gem into the source of all good qualities.

I'll now give some answers
To the questions of this great Bön priest:

My homeland is Tsa Rön on Gungthang plain.
I went to Ü and Tsang to study.
In youth I destroyed my hated enemies
With evil powers, curses, and hail.

Afterwards I felt intense regret
And went to Marpa the translator.
Receiving Dharma, I made practice my sole concern
And slashed through confusion about the natural state.
With realization of actual state born within,
I've now no fear even of death.

My sight is on reality;
I cultivate currents, channels, and drops.
I practice in the state of reality—
The three spontaneous bodies my result.

My lama is Marpa Lotsawa,
Whose lineage extends through Tilopa and Nāropa

Reaching to conqueror Vajradhara.
I took up practice of Ear-Whispered Tantras,[39]
And thus obtained mastery of currents and channels.

The Bön priest broke in, "I'm amazed! And what do you Dharma practitioners have to say about the Bön religion, the ultimate swastika (i.e.,
reality)?"

Mila continued:

> Listen Bön teacher—I'll settle your doubts,
> Your cage of delusion and wrong thinking.
>
> First, concerning the source of Dharma,
> He is called Buddha
> Who developed illuminating gnosis
> Through elimination of all illusion.
>
> Buddha is without beginning or end—
> The primal buddha[40] is without cause—
> This is often stated in scriptural sources.
> Beings are ignorant from the beginning,
> Amassing action through such ignorance.
> They take on bodies accordingly,
> And as before, amass various actions
> With this newly acquired body.
>
> Action is threefold—good, bad, and mixed.
> Of actions induced by the three poisons
> Hatred yields birth in hell,
> Desire yields birth as a frustrated spirit,
> And delusion yields animal birth.
> Mixed action produces diverse results within those states.
>
> Good action yields higher states,
> And supremely good action
> Increases the stores of merit and gnosis.
> Giving, morality, and patience
> Are the source of merit;

And concentration and wisdom,
In divine or human lives,
Are the source of great gnosis.

However, concentration not imbued with
Pure wisdom, no matter how good,
Yields the four absorptions and four media
Up to the peak of existence.[41]
Once karmic results are exhausted therein,
One wanders again in samsara.

Effort assists them all:[42]
And the state of gnosis is perfected
By integration of concentration and wisdom
Through realization of the natural state as it really is.

The results of completing the two stores
Of merit and gnosis in this way
Consist of the sky-like dharma-body for oneself,
Resulting from pure gnosis,
The enjoyment-body like a sun in the sky
For the training of developed disciples,
And the emanation-body like sunbeams
For training undeveloped companions,
Both resulting from the store of merit.

This configuration is called
"Resultant spontaneous three bodies";
Such a little tidbit of teaching
Is a small part of the Dharma system.

In the nonsense of fools of earlier times
Bön and Dharma are called elder and younger brothers.
The reason for this explained
By earlier Bönpos is as follows:

"In the beginning was neither earth nor sky.
Water, fire, and air likewise didn't exist.

From this primordial void state
Bön-mother 'Space-Treasury' in anger
Exhaled the air element from her mouth,
Emitted the water element as urine,
And flashed forth fire from the heat of her mind.

"She compacted teeth and fingernails into earth foundation
Upon which the egg of existence was self-born,
And from the cracking of the shell of this egg
The six states of being, the apparent world, and Bön itself arose."

They claim Dharma arose after Bön!
For this reason they are elder and younger brothers
According to the nonsense of these fools.

In the beginning sky didn't exist.
Sky is equivalent to *space*.
Space is naturally empty
And cannot be said to exist or not.

A "space-mother" within this primal void
Is also the nonsense of fools—
Cover your ears with your hands
At the sound of such nonsense.

According to more modern sources
A very clever Buddhist pandit
In the land of India
Visited the house of a whore.

Arising before dawn, he dressed,
But by mistake wrapped himself
In the woman's skirt instead of his own.

Returning to the monastery at dawn,
He was seen wearing the blue skirt
And expelled from the community.

He made his way eventually to Tibet

And with hard feelings in this land of exile
Created a perverse religion and named it Bön.
At that time in Upper Tibet[43]
A son was born to a woman
By a great and powerful black nāga.

He had very large ears
And was thus known
By the name Baby Donkey-man.

Although he was son of a powerful nāga,
His mother was of Bön religion,
And so the boy when grown
Was also learned in Bön
And called Donkey-man Shenrab.[44]

Then having heard of the fame
Of Bön teacher Blue Skirt,
Shenrab went to him across the vast northern plain.

This modern lineage of Bön
Extends back only to Blue Skirt and Shenrab.
Thus if you think: "If they both lead to the ultimate,
What's the difference between Dharma and Bön?"
I'll reply that the ancestry of Bön
Is religion perverter, powerful nāga, and demons—
How could it lead to the ultimate?

Thus Bön has inferior ancestry,
And like all "outsider" religions
Diverges from Dharma in sources of refuge:
The Triple Gem is the refuge for Buddhists,
While it is Brahmā, Īśvara, and Viṣṇu for outsiders.

The perfect buddha is one
Able to liberate others
Through his own freedom from samsara;
But worldly gods like Īśvara,
Still bound to samsara themselves,

Are able to grant
Only temporal siddhis—
How could they grant the freedom of liberation?
That's why they're called "outsiders."

It's true that those who practice Bön
Can indeed cure sickness, remove obstructions,
And gain ordinary siddhis.
The numerous Bönpo siddhas
Ride drums through the sky,
Burn great fires on water,
Cut iron with a feather, and so on.
But if you think these are signs of development,
I'll explain it like this:

Meditation on the empty, illusory, superficial world
Will turn out accordingly—
Haven't you heard of becoming a tiger
By visualizing your body as a tiger?

Meditation on earth, air, fire, and water
Also produces like results,
But the root of this illusion
Is slashed only by a buddha—
No one else can destroy illusion.

Thus the true path is traveled
When practicing the teachings of the undeluded Buddha—
Buddhahood's not attained any other way.

If one is limited to achieving siddhis,
How can one reach the ultimate
By Hindu, Bön, or other ways?
And if flying in the sky is sufficient
All birds would be buddhas!

Therefore, all of these
Are just signs of mundane attainment

Of a superficial, illusory nature
Unable to lead one to enlightenment.
When *everything* is meditated as *totally* void
To gain realization of voidness
And slash mental delusion
About illusion existing from beginningless time,
It induces nihilism which causes low states
And cannot prevent the increase of misery.
Moreover, desire for siddhis is materialism,
Which also binds one to samsara.

Thus if you would enter the unmistaken path,
The two realities should be known:
The superficial world and the absolute.

The superficial is also twofold:
False and unreal
And conditionally real.

The former, the false superficial—
Like a reflection in water or mirror—
Isn't taken as real even by worldly children.
The latter, all apparent phenomena—
Which till nirvana's attained
Appear to be real—
Are thus superficially real.

To realize absolute reality,
Remove the obstructions of action and affliction
By compiling a great store of merit
Through giving, morality, patience, and effort.
And remove the obstruction to omniscience
By concentration well imbued with wisdom.

Then by integrating pure quiescence and insight,
Absolute reality is confronted.
That's the way of realization for yogi-repas.

Mila's detailed explanation of these points through the medium of his eloquent speech inspired firm faith in his listeners. Approaching Jetsün the Bön priest renounced the Bön religion and asked for empowerment and instruction. He set his sights on the goal of reality and after completing the developmental process became known as an excellent, expert meditator.

Mila meeting the "dream" shepherdess

17

Mila's Journey Inspired by a Dream

AFTER TRAINING THE PEOPLE OF LOWO and the herdsmen that autumn, the great lord of yogis decided to head in the direction of Kuthang plain. He said to Seben and the other repas, "You go to the lowlands and make one round of begging. When winter comes, resume your practice in White Rock Horse Tooth Cave. I'm going to Kuthang plain at the instigation of a dream last night."

They begged him, "Please take us along."

He replied, "If we all went, there'd be no chance to get winter provisions. You go to White Rock—your practice will develop there." And to advise them he sang this song:

> I pray at the feet of my lama.
>
> Faithful Seben, respectful and so devoted,
> Broad minded, well intended, in accord with all,
> Vigorous and diligent in practice—
> Though you're a young repa,
> You are a son lovingly nourished by me.
> You're a precious son dear to my heart,
> A wealthy son, heir to my precepts,
> An able son who bears the burden,
> A fortunate son with a foothold on the path.
> Listen now, faithful one:
>
> We were born alone;
> We will die alone—by ourselves—
> Who has the power to stay forever?
> Now while we have the chance,
> Let's each practice by ourselves.
>
> We will see who has the greater realization,
> Who has more endurance and wisdom,
> Who's better at practicing Dharma.

All you young repas
Practice as Seben directs.
Sit tight on your cushions.

So they descended to Gungthang plain while Mila headed toward
Kuthang. After passing through Thang and Khum,[45] he met up with a
patron. Mila asked him, "Can you give any food to this yogi?"

He replied, "My own place is in the lowlands. I'm just here on business.
Where are you from, yogi? You don't look the same as other Dharma practitioners. How come?"

Mila sang this song in reply:

Homage to the holy lamas.

Listen patron-questioner:
I am Milarepa.
I'm an ascetic beggar,
An expert meditator, seeker of alms,
One who accepts what comes my way.

Listen, I'll explain why
My ways are different than others':

Others attend to the business of *this* life;
I concern myself with *future* lives.

Others seek a pleasing mate;
I'd only be troubled by a wife.

Others seek status in this life
I always maintain a humble position.

Others adorn themselves with clothes and ornaments;
I wear a ragged robe, no ornaments.

Others try to make their bodies sexy;
I just act easy and natural.

Others seek delicious food and drink;
I find my food like a bird.[46]

Do you understand this, questioner?

The patron exclaimed, "You're yogi Mila! I didn't know it was you! " He paid respects and asked for blessings, and then said, "My name is Gureb Darma Gyel. Why don't you come to my place?"

Mila didn't do so, but went on to Naphu. The patron supplied him with provisions for three months, and in return Mila taught him much Dharma. One day Mila told him, "Now, I'm going to an isolated place," and not listening to the patron's entreaties, he set out. At the approach to a pass he met a nomad and asked, "Is there a comfortable cave in this direction?"

He replied, "Across this pass, on the north slope of the mountain, there's a cave called Pong Lung."

Deciding to go there, Mila passed through a canyon at the far side of the pass where a shepherdess was grazing goats and sheep. As he approached her, she said:

What kind of man do I see?
I see a naked ascetic.
I see a shameless man.
I see a man unaffected by hunger and cold.
Don't stay here—go to Grey Rock—
You'll surely achieve your goal.

Having said this, she and all her herd vanished like a rainbow. Mila went and stayed at Grey Rock Vajra Stronghold. There he consumed the food of absorption, donned the cloak of austerities, and sat under the overhang of his cave as a man wears a hat. His mental power and clear illumination grew stronger there, and he sang this song:

Homage to the feet of my father-lama.

I, the yogi Milarepa,
Offer this song in the natural state,

Dancing and singing in the realm of great bliss.
Listen, mother and host of ḍākinīs.

This fearlessness of heat and cold
Isn't matched by ordinary faith.

This ability to focus myself in isolation
Isn't equaled by ordinary concentration.

This equanimity free of objective projections
Isn't matched by any ordinary view.

This inexpressible post-attainment
Isn't equaled by ordinary meditation.

This consistent awareness
Isn't matched by ordinary practice.

This integration of voidness and compassion
Isn't equaled by ordinary achievements.

This robe of freedom from cold
Isn't matched by ordinary clothes.

This concentration free of hunger
Is unequaled by ordinary meat and beer.

This draught at the stream of enlightenment
Isn't matched by ordinary drink.

This satisfaction born within
Isn't equaled by ordinary treasure.

The translator Marpa Lotsawa
Isn't equaled by ordinary siddhas.

This sight of one's own mind as deity's face
Is unequaled by ordinary personal deities.

This illusory-body free of ills
Is far better than ordinary medicines.

This yogi Milarepa
Isn't equaled by ordinary meditators.

Are you happy, yogi?
Listen further, host of ḍākinīs:
In Grey Rock Vajra Stronghold Cave
I sought the vajra-like concentration.[47]

This birthless clear light of mind-itself
Imbued with voidness and compassion
I now understand to be samsara
For the unrealized, while for the realized
It shines as dharma-body.

I now understand the manifestation
Of holy dharma-body for my own welfare
In birthless, deathless reality,
Brilliant, clear, free from taint.

Driven by love and compassion
For those who haven't realized
Such a natural state as this,
I dedicate all actions for others' welfare
With strong desire for their liberation.
I've now manifested my form-body
Providing others' welfare according to their needs.

"Death" is just a preconception;
I've realized preconception to be dharma-body
Free from birth, free from death.

Wondrous! Wondrous! Samsaric things
Don't exist, yet appear! Great wonder!

I offer this song of worship, holy lama!
Share in this feast of sound, host of ḍākinīs!

He pressed on in practice. One day patron Darma Gyel arrived carrying a bag of flour and a side of meat, saying, "I've been looking for you a long time! I've brought flour and provisions." After looking around he said, "There's not even a rain basin in that rock pile outside. You must have had a lot of trouble."

In reply Mila sang:

> To great translator Marpa,
> Holy, precious, qualified lama,
> I constantly pray—
> Protect me with unwavering attention.
>
> Listen now, faithful patron:
> What was unclear is clear—
> This clear light is illumination.
>
> What was not warm is warm—
> This scant cotton robe is warmth.
>
> What was not blissful is blissful—
> This illusory body is bliss.
>
> What was not joyful is joyful—
> This dream is joy.
>
> Are you happy, yogi?
> Is Grey Rock Vajra Cave high or not?
>
> If Grey Rock were not high
> How could vultures soar beneath it?
>
> If this cliff edge were not cold,
> How could streams and rivers freeze?
>
> If I were not warmed by *tummo* bliss,
> How could a cotton robe keep me warm?
>
> If I didn't eat the food of concentration,
> How could I endure hunger without provisions?

If I didn't imbibe the stream of enlightenment,
How could I endure thirst without water?

If lama's precepts were not profound,
How could they conquer devils and obstructions?

If this yogi were not realized,
How could he stay in desolate mountains?

Through the kindness of my skillful lama
I've made practice my chief concern.

How could one who takes all things as friends
Find anything unfavorable?

Pleased to meet you again, Darma Gyel.

This patron came another time bringing supplies, but he found the interior of the cave completely flooded with water. Remembering his lama, he wept and went away. Local people told him that Mila was still living there so he went back to find out. He found instead that the interior of the cave was ablaze with fire. Praying for his lama he left. The people again insisted that he was there, so he went back and found the cave itself completely gone. The thought occurred to him that he was unable to find Mila due to a great karmic obstruction, so he stayed there and prayed with intense longing for three days. Then in the morning, a white reliquary appeared. He paid respects to the reliquary and circled it, praying. Then three days later in the early morning he found that the reliquary had changed into the Jetsün Lama. In joy he paid respects and touched Mila's feet. "Why have I been unable to find you for so long?" Mila sang:

To my holy lama Vajradhara,
Revered Lotsawa who revealed
The essence of birthless mahāmudrā,
I pray—grant me blessings.

I will answer your question,
Faithful patron—listen carefully:

To Grey Rock Vajra Stronghold Cave
I, the Tibetan Milarepa,
Came to meditate directed by ḍākinīs.
Many experiences and realizations dawned
And now I've seen my mind's true essence,
But I'll not reveal these secrets now.

Patron, when you came before
While I was focused
In the saturative concentration of water,[48]
You found the cave was filled with water.

Later you found my fire saturation,
Then my saturation of air,
And finally that white reliquary
Appeared when I was focused
In the saturative concentration of earth.

When your karmic obstruction was removed,[49] you saw me.
Keep a tight lip—don't tell others.

All appearances are false.
False appearances are the mandala of illusion,
But for the unrealized they seem conditionally real.

Do you understand this, Darma Gyel?
Mila's goal is spontaneously achieved—
A great opportunity for followers
Like Darma Gyel to enter the path.

He was overwhelmed. That winter Mila taught him the five stages,[50] and through good realization experience he gained a foothold on the path.

Mila amidst a rainbow aura

18

Is Milarepa Dying?

THE GREAT LORD OF YOGIS, JETSÜN MILAREPA, was staying in the glorious palace of Chu Bar teaching Dharma to some disciples. Right at sunrise of the eighth day of the month Jetsün elevated himself three stories into the air and sat there cross-legged in the midst of a rainbow aura.

His disciples knelt in reverence, and after a moment, little by little, he sank down. At this they thought, "Is he dying?" They wept and lamented, and some of them like Shengom Repa said:

> Precious siddha-yogi,
> Sitting amidst your body's rainbow aura,
> Absorbed in the realm of space,
> And vanished from the range of our sight,
> Is this true or is it false?
> Is it real or is it illusion?
> Precious Jetsün Lama,
> Pray remain for the sake of beings.

They begged him like this, mourning profusely. After a moment he elevated himself again to a height of one spear's length and sang this song:

> I bow to the feet of translator Marpa,
> Outstanding man of Lhodrak
> Who fulfills the hopes of his trainees—
> Grant me your constant blessings.
>
> Through the kindness of my unique father-lama
> All appearances were experienced as mind,
> Mind itself realized as baseless, rootless,
> Consciousness purified in the state of gnosis,
> And samsara and nirvana known to be nondual.

Buddha and *beings* are merely names—
In actuality don't exist at all.
Nonexistent, and yet they appear.
The mistake results from ignorant action—
Attached to illusion they are beings,
Freed from illusion they are buddhas.

Eh ma! Yogis gathered here,
Look into the sphere of birthless mind!
Let dawn the enjoyment of ceaseless play!
When free of hope and fear—that's the result.
Why speak of birth and death?
Come to the natural, unmodified state!

Vast ceiling of sky
Suddenly pierced by a rabbit's horn!

Banner of changeless dharma-body
Held in the hand of a barren woman's son!

Eh ma! All things of samsara and nirvana
Don't exist—yet appear—
Appear—yet are void—why?

When I was focused a bit
In space saturation,[51]
Why did you senselessly mourn?

When mind and space are united
Through union of body and mind,
Dharma-body is revealed
And desired goals attained.
Why so unhappy at that?

Therefore, you don't comprehend Dharma.
You think I'd abandon others' welfare—
But I reached the royal station of dharma-body for myself
Through the force of expansive supplication

For spontaneous achievement of others' welfare
By the union of voidness and compassion.

My twofold form-body for others' sake
Will reappear till samsara's emptied,
An uninterrupted flow of help for beings
Like a wish-granting gem
Or divinely worshipped wishing tree
For those who need training, wherever they may be.

"Furthermore, I—your old father—have shown you the essence of the true natural state. I've punctured the myth of samsara, crushed the hidden core of illusion, and split samsara and nirvana apart. I offered you buddha in the palm of my hand. What more could you want? But still you lounge back into samsara. You were praying and lamenting out of attachment to illusory appearances. Phooey!

"At the end of life comes death; at the end of composition comes dispersion. In view of your prayers I'll remain a few years longer, but I can't stay forever. So now's the time to slash your doubts about my precepts, those of you who need to do so.

"Then, after falling asleep with great bliss in the space-bed of reality, I'll provide for the welfare of other trainees. What's the need for mourning this? You must make effort in cultivating intense compassion, the mind aimed at enlightenment, and expansive supplication as long as life lasts for the sake of beings lost in samsara, overcome with its miseries."

I pray at the feet of holy Marpa,
Precious translator imbued with kindness,
Who provides help for other beings,
Unswayed from his dharma-body state.
Grant blessings to gain a foothold on the path
To myself, my followers,
And all living beings.

Listen awhile, faithful ones:
If you don't meditate on rare leisure and opportunity,
You'll be unable to keep morality pure.

If you don't meditate on impermanence and death,
There's danger of involvement in "permanent" life-schemes.

If you don't carefully consider action and result,
There's danger of disregarding cause and effect.

If you don't take refuge in the Triple Gem,
There's danger of wandering lower states of samsara.

If you don't persevere in compiling the two stores,
There's danger of staying lost in illusion.

If you don't regard all beings as parents,
There's danger of being a Disciple or Rhino.[52]

If you don't overflow with love and compassion,
There's danger of aversion and hatred.

If quiescence's not born in mind,
There's danger of being blown by winds of distraction.

If mind's lucidity isn't kept clear,
There's danger of being led to animal states.

If recollective, critical awareness isn't maintained,
There's danger of sinking in the mud of depression.

If you don't persevere in engaging objectives,
There's danger of being blown by winds of excitement.

If the eight corrective factors aren't applied,
There's danger of succumbing to five faults of concentration.[53]

If not well equipped with analytic wisdom,
There's danger of straying into the absorptions.

If fabrication isn't slashed by insight,
There's danger of spinning in samsara forever.

Therefore, with the force of faith
Meditate lama, personal deity, and Triple Gem
Dwelling inseparably on the crown of your head,
And by fervent prayer in four sessions each day
Receive their blessings in mind and illumine it with realization.

In isolated mountain regions
Cultivate the unmeditative, undistracted state.
Realization experience will be born within;
Warmth of bliss will blaze in body.

Don't go begging for the sake of food—
Eat stones and drink water of austerity![54]
Positive qualities will be born within,
And you'll have confidence of impartiality.

When you've obtained keen skill in objectives,[55]
Then bliss-warmth of *tummo* burns in your body,
And when you've obtained mastery of currents and channels,
Developmental signs and qualities will be born,
And this mere cotton robe will be enough.

Come to the undistracted realm
Of birthless mahāmudrā —
Mind will attain its invincible state,
And the goal be spontaneously achieved.

Do you understand this, yogis?
Receive this song of worship, precious lama.
Share in this feast of sound, host of dākinīs.
Remove your obstructions, nonhumans.

Closing Verse

I'm a yogi who wanders the countryside,
A beggar who travels alone,
A pauper who's got nothing.

I left behind the land of my birth,
Turned my back on my own fine house,
And gave up my fertile fields.

I stayed in isolated mountain retreats,
Practiced in rock caves surrounded by snow,
And found food as birds do—
That's how its been up to now.

There's no telling the day of my death,
But I have a purpose before I die.
That's the story of me, the yogi;
Now I'll give *you* some advice:

Trying to control the events of this life,
Trying and trying to be so clever,
Always planning to manipulate your world,
Involved in repetitive social relations—
In the midst of these preparations for the future
You arrive unaware at your final years,
Not realizing your brow is knit with wrinkles,
Not knowing your hair is turned white,
Not seeing the skin of your eyes sink down,
Not admitting the sag of your mouth and nose.

Even while chased by the envoys of death
You still sing and rejoice in pleasure.
Not knowing if life will last till morning,
You still make plans for tomorrow's future.

Not knowing where rebirth will occur,
You still maintain a complacent contentment.
Now's the time to get ready for death—
That's my sincere advice to you;
If its import strikes you, start your practice.

Notes

1. The quotations in this chapter are from "Mila's First Meditation," "Rechungpa's Mahāmudrā Pride," "Six Secret Songs," and "Mila Teaches Two Scholars How to Practice," all from *Stories and Songs from the Oral Tradition.* Complete translations of these songs are included in the second volume of this work, *Miraculous Journey* (Lotsawa, 1986), available from Wisdom Publications.

2. The fourth body is the essential-body, representing the unity of the dharma-body, enjoyment-body, and emanation-body.

3. The mentally controlled body of an accomplished yogi.

4. "Diamond Sow," a female tantric deity.

5. See song number 8, "Rechungpa's Confusion."

6. Refers to the visualization of Vajra Varāhī, the "Diamond Sow," during the first phase of *tummo*, the yoga of external heat. The subsequent lines deal with generation of the inner heat.

7. The hundred-syllable Vajrasattva mantra employed for purification.

8. The fluids or "drops" (*bindu*).

9. The complete Tibetan title is: *rje btsun mi la ras pai rdo rjei mgyur druk sogs gsung rgyun thor bu pa 'ga'.* It was compiled and printed at Tashi Khyil (*bkra shis 'khyil*) Monastery, Amdo, Tibet.

10. This refers to the process of identification of body and mind with one's personal deity who then makes offerings to other deities. Their acceptance of the offering is visualized by the tubes extending from their mouths to the offering.

11. Don't be inattentive and miss the teachings, like a pot turned upside down. Don't forget what you've heard, like a cracked and leaking pot. Don't taint the teachings with preconceived ideas, like a dirty pot.

12. Made from the concentrated essences of herbs. They are sometimes used by yogis to maintain vigor during long periods of meditation without food.

13. Faith, morality, modesty, receptiveness to Dharma, attentiveness, charity, and wisdom.

14. Bodhicitta, or "mind-for-enlightenment," here stands for the white drop of semen and refers to the practice of "stoppage."

15. When mind is overly scattered or distracted by objects, it can be corrected by detaching it through mental technique like that of a raven, which when caged on an oceangoing boat struggles to be free, but when freed escapes the boat only to return when it finds nowhere to alight.

16. Jowo Rinpoche (*Jo bo rin po che*) in Kyirong (*skyid rong*) in what is now the Yambu region of Nepal.

17. This is aimed at certain meditators who mistake developed quiescence for insight. See the introduction.

18. Literally, Kagyu (*bka' brgyud*)—the name of Mila's sect.

19. That is, the highest level of concentrative absorption of the samsaric mind.

20. Possessed only by a perfect buddha.

21. A doctrine brought to Tibet by Atiśa. The small personality is motivated toward happiness in this and future lives, the middling personality toward personal liberation from the miseries of samsara, and the great personality toward freeing oneself and all beings. The practices listed in this verse apply to them in different ways.

22. Breath or wind, bile, and phlegm.

23. The former is defined as avoidance of evil through reference to one's own judgment, the latter avoidance of evil through reference to others' judgment.

24. Medicine, logic, language, crafts, and spiritual knowledge.

25. The *upāsaka* vows of abstinence from killing, stealing, lying, sexual misconduct, and personal adornments.

26. The path of method consists of yogic practices aimed at developing control of the psycho-physical currents and the powers associated with such control.

27. Fabrication (*prapañca*) means the stream of mental elaboration of reality that ignorant beings take as the real world. It is the inner flow

of discursiveness on both unconscious (preconceptive) and conscious (inner monologue) levels. The four extremes are belief in existence, nonexistence, both, and neither.

28. Refers to the practice of holding pebbles in the mouth during meditation to allay hunger.

29. Unusual reference to the tantric practice of consuming the "five unclean substances" after they are yogically transformed into nectar.

30. The mantric seed-syllable of Tummo Yoga (see glossary).

31. These are the three "baskets" (*piṭaka*) into which the Buddha's actual teachings are arranged. They are discourses (*sūtra*), mental science (*abhidharma*), and discipline (*vinaya*).

32. The three commitments are the vow of personal liberation, the bodhisattva vow, and the tantric vow.

33. This could be a reference to the famous Kadampa Geshe Tönba (*dge bshes ston pa*) who was extensively involved in establishing monasteries and Dharma centers, or it could merely be a generic reference to the title meaning "spiritual friend."

34. The seventh of the fourteen major lapses in Mantrayāna is revealing tantric secrets to those unfit to hear them.

35. Refers to the tantric manner of developing the mind-for-enlightenment as white bindu in the head center that must be "melted" and "dripped" into the central nāḍī. If one attempts to incorporate afflictive emotions into the path before this, it will only yield negative and even harmful results.

36. This is Sangye Gyap (*sangs rgyad skyaps*) Repa of Ragma, mentioned in the *Autobiography* and *Hundred Thousand Songs*.

37. Lowo (*glo bo sman thang*) is the area in Nepal now known as Mustang.

38. The *Hundred Thousand Songs,* chapter 20, "Milarepa's Meeting with Kar Chung Repa." In this version the disciple only pretends to be ill. Mila sings the songs "Right Yoga Practice," "Song of Transcience with Eight Similes," and "Ten Difficulties." He thus converts Kar Chung Repa (*mkar chung*), who later became one of his close disciples, and takes him along to Ti Se.

39. The *Ḍākinīkarṇatantras.*

40. For the Kagyu sect the primal buddha (*adibuddha*) is Vajradhara.

41. That is, the highest state of concentrative absorption of the samsaric mind.

42. Effort is the fourth of the six transcendences, the other five being giving, morality, patience, concentration, and wisdom mentioned above.

43. The regions of Ngari (*mnga' ris*) and modern Ladakh. The Bön themselves consider their religion to have originated in these parts.

44. The Bön consider Shenrab (*gshen rabs*) to be the original human founder of their religion.

45. Probably Thangboche and Sharkumbu (*thang po che, shar khums bu*) in northern Nepal.

46. In Tibet this expression indicates being happy with whatever one can get.

47. *Vajropamasamadhi*, the concentration immediately imminent to enlightenment.

48. The saturative concentrations are one of the yogic means for gaining control of perception; the meditator produces a visual perception of one of the elements or primary colors strong enough to overlay or saturate his ordinary perception of things. That the patron was affected by this indicates the great intensity of Mila's concentration.

49. By his grief and efforts to find Mila.

50. The *Pañcakrama*, another formulation of the tantric path in terms of stages.

51. See note 48.

52. *Śrāvaka* and *Pratyekabuddha*. The pratyeka, or solitary buddhas, are called rhinoceros-like because of their aversion to the company of even a buddha. They are both realized beings of the small vehicle.

53. This song is a brief "stages of the path" teaching in precept form. The section beginning five verses back deals with the process of developing quiescence. Depression and excitement simply refer to the state of mental sluggishness and unresponsiveness, and that of mental over-responsiveness, which disrupts stabilization on the objective. The five faults and eight corrective factors in producing quiescence: 1) laziness: corrected by faith, aspiration, effort, practical intensity; 2) forgetfulness (of precepts): corrected by recollective awareness; 3) depression and excitement: corrected by critical

awareness; 4) not producing corrective factors: corrected by producing corrective factors; 5) producing unnecessary factors: corrected by focusing on the object.

54. See note 28.

55. That is, in the process of meditation on the graded objectives of quiescence and insight.

Glossary

absorption, absorption levels (*dhyāna*)   The distinct, meta-stable states of mental operation attained through the quieting of mental functioning by one-pointed concentration. Attainment of the eight successively more quiescent absorption levels—the first four comprising the form realm and the second four the formless realm—involves the suppression of thought and disturbing mental functions. Their duration depends on the force of the process of suppression. They are states common to all yoga and are entirely samsaric in nature.

action (*karma*)   Exactly that; any intentional or unintentional act performed through the "three doors," that is, body, speech, and mind. There are three types: virtuous, yielding positive results; evil, yielding negative results; and fixed, which refers to action in a state of absorption which yields results that are "fixed" or limited to the absorption levels.

afflictions (*kleśa*)   Mental functions that are obstructive to the quiescence of nirvana. There are six primary afflictions: ignorance, desire, aversion, doubt, pride, and wrong views; and a number of subsidiary afflictions associated with their occurrence.

analytic insight (*vipaśyanā*)   The process of detailed examination of the meditation object as to its actual mode of existence. It involves thought and is aimed at penetrating the conceptual process. It results in receptivity to the direct perception of voidness.

anti-god (*asura*)   *See* states, six.

appearances, apparent world (Tib. *snang ba*)   Reality as it appears to a common individual whose conditioned, distorted perception experiences reality in the form of discrete, independent identities. Synonym: illusory world, superficial reality.

bardo   The state of consciousness between death and rebirth.

bodies, three (*trikāya*)   The three modes of existence and communication for an enlightened being. The dharma-body (*dharmakāya*) is the embodiment of voidness and its realization, the enjoyment-body (*sambhogakāya*) is the means of communication with advanced meditators, and the emanation-body (*nirmāṇakāya*) appears like a physical body in the world, but its form and activities are consciously directed and consist of the training of undeveloped beings. A fourth body, the essential-body (*svabhāvakāya*) represents the unity of the above three.

Bön   The native religion of Tibet. Its followers are called Bönpo.

centers (*cakra*)   The foci of the flow of current (*prāṇa*) in the psycho-physiological system of tantric yoga. They are located at the head, throat, heart, and navel.

channels (*nāḍī*)   Pathways along which the currents (*prāṇa*) move. The main channels are the *avadhūtī* (central channel), and the *ida,* and *pingala* (left and right channels).

circle feast (Tib. *tshogs 'khor*)   A feast of offering attended by the host of ḍākinīs.

clear light (Tib. *od gsal;* Skt. *ābhāsvarā*)   The experience of the natural, primal,unmodified state of the mind.

completion phase   *See* phases, two.

currents (*prāṇa*)   The psycho-physical forces of the mind, body, and environment.

ḍākinīs   Female tantric deities who aid the yogi and oversee his practice and behavior.

dedication (*parināma*)   The sharing with others of one's virtuous actions, successful practice, and attainment. It consists of prayer, visualization, and attitude that should close each practice session, and also includes the dedication customarily given by yogis in return for food.

devils, four (*māra*)   Samsaric enemies to liberation; they are one's psycho-physical constituents, afflictive mental states, death, and external obstructions.

dharma-body (*dharmakāya*)   *See* bodies, three.

dharma-realm, dharma-element (*dharmadhātu*)   The ultimate reality of all things.

disciple (*śrāvaka*)   The disciples of Buddha Shakyamuni and the followers of their schools. There were eighteen such schools in India whose teachings comprise the Small Vehicle. Specifically it refers to persons who have attained arhatship.

drops (*bindu*)   "Substances" of the yogic psycho-physical system. In tantra the white bindu, or white element, is equivalent to the mind-for-enlightenment. It must be "melted" at the head center and "dripped" down the central channel to the lower centers, producing the four ecstasies.

ego (*ātman*)   The imagined self or identity of persons (personal ego) and things (phenomenal ego), which are inherently lacking any independent identity.

elements, four (*dhātu*)   Earth (solidity), water (fluidity), fire (heat), and air (motility). Space is sometimes counted as a fifth element.

emanation-body (*nirmanakāya*)   *See* bodies, three.

enjoyment-body (*sambhogakāya*)   *See* bodies, three.

enlightenment (*bodhi*)   The state of buddhahood constituted by perfection of the two stores and removal of the two obscurations. It is the only level of attainment beyond the range of samsara.

enlightenment-mind   *See* mind-for-enlightenment.

essential-body (*svabhāvakāya*)   *See* bodies, three.

evils, ten (*akuśala*)   The ten main evils are killing, stealing, sexual misconduct, lying, slander, abusive speech, senseless speech, coveting, ill will, and wrong views. The ten main virtues are abstaining from these evils.

fabrication (*prapañca*)   The internal stream of conceptualization directed by imprinted preconceptions. The term includes both the internal flow of thought constructs and the self and environment resulting from them.

food of absorption, food of concentration   Nourishment during meditative states derived from concentrative absorption. It can sustain the yogi in place of food for periods of time.

frustrated spirits (*preta*)   *See* states, six.

fundamental consciousness (*ālayavijñāna*)   The eighth consciousness, according to the Mind-Only system developed by Asaṅga in the fifth century. It is the basic substratum of the individual's consciousness that carries the imprintings of "seeds" of past and future experiences.

geshe (*kalyāṇamitra*) "Spiritual friend"; a title given to a person who has demonstrated exceptional competence in the scriptures and subjects of basic Buddhism.

gnosis (*jñāna*) Generally, knowledge; specifically, the wisdom by which the apparent world and its reality are simultaneously perceived.

Great Vehicle (*Mahāyāna*) *See* vehicle.

higher states (*sugati*) *See* states, six.

identity (*svabhāva*) The "intrinsic identifiability" of anything. The ordinary mind compartmentalizes its experience into objects appearing as independent entities. The inherent lack of identity in persons and things constitutes voidness, which is their true mode of existence.

illusory, illusion (*māyopama, bhrānti*) Mayopama, "like a (magical) illusion" (*maya-upama*), emphasizes the fact that the mind distorts experience of reality in the way a magician alters our perceptions. Our conditioned perception causes the world to appear as something it is not.

illusory-body The mentally controlled body of an accomplished yogi. (When unhyphenated it indicates the ordinary body of an undeveloped being that takes its form through deluded preconceptions). Synonym: rainbow-body, vajra-body.

imprint (*vāsanā*) The mental traces of past experience and action that give rise to the present samsaric situation.

infinitudes, four (*apramāṇa*) Basic emotions that can be developed into catalysts for generating the mind aimed at enlightenment (*bodhicitta*). They are love, compassion, joy, and mental equanimity.

insight *See* analytic insight.

karmamudrā Refers to the practice of sexual union in tantric yoga.

lower states (*durgati*) *See* states, six.

mahāmudrā "Great Gesture" or "Great Seal." An advanced practice closely aligned with the Peerless (*anuttara*) Yoga Tantras; aimed at direct revelation of the natural reality of the apparent world.

mandala (*maṇḍala*) The symbolic, graphic representation of a tantric deity's realm of existence. Also, the arrangement of offerings in tantric ritual (*pūjā*).

mantra Sound in the form of syllables and words that can communicate the realities of tantric deities, grant supernormal powers (*siddhi*), or induce purification and realization.

Mantra Vehicle (*Mantrayāna*)   *See* vehicle.

method (*upāya*)   The active expression of the mind-for-enlightenment (*bodhicitta*). It is the complement of transcendent wisdom that balances its intense revelations and what the bodhisattva uses to relate to beings, skillfully turning each situation into an opportunity for advancement for all.

mind-for-enlightenment (*bodhicitta*)   The intent to attain one's own enlightenment in order to help liberate others. It is not the state of enlightenment itself, but the selfless drive to attain it for the sake of others. In the Great Vehicle it is the necessary complement to the penetrating insight into voidness and in the Tantric Vehicle the prerequisite to real practice.

nāga   Fabulous human-headed serpents of Indian mythology who dwell under water in their own advanced civilization.

natural state (Tib. *gnas lugs*)   The natural mode of existence of all things; the mental state wherein experience is not distorted by preconceived perceptions of identities.

nirvana (*nirvāṇa*)   The cessation of one's own misery through eradication of afflictional mental states. In the Great Vehicle nirvana is used in distinction to enightenment, which involves not only the eradication of misery but also the attainment of unique abilities and insights into reality.

non-identification (*niravalamba*)   In gnostic wisdom, the perception free from the preconceptual conditionings that "create" the discrete, independent identities of the apparent world.

obscurations, two (*avaraṇa*)   The afflictional obscuration (*kleśāvaraṇa*) consists of negative mental states that obscure nirvana's freedom from misery. The objective obscuration (*jñeyāvaraṇa*) consists of fundamental misperceptions of the world that obscure perfect enlightenment.

phases, two (*krama*)   The two stages of tantric practice. The first, the production phase (*utpattikrama*), involves the visualized production of the tantric deities and their domains. The second, the completion phase (*utpannakrama*), is the completion of this process by perceiving the voidness of all appearances.

poisons, three or five (*visa*)   The principal afflictive mental functions: ignorance, desire, aversion, as well as jealousy and pride.

post-attainment   The state immediately following any direct, transcendent experience of voidness, called "actual realization state." During the actual realization state the perception of the apparent world yields to the perception of its voidness, while in the post-attainment state the preconceived perception of the apparent world returns subtly altered by the preceding experience.

preta   "Frustrated spirit."   *See also* states, six.

production phase   *See* phases, two.

quiescence (*śamatha*)   The systematic quieting of mental activity through practice of one-pointed concentration. It is the means of attaining the eight absorption levels and the prerequisite for proper practice of analytic insight.

realities, two (*satyadvaya*)   The two modes of existence of phenomena. The superficial reality (*saṁvṛtisatya*) is the world appearing in the form of independent identities to ordinary, undefective perception conditioned by preconceptions. Absolute reality (*paramārthasatya*) is the voidness of all phenomena, that is, their inherent lack of independent identity.

realms of existence, six   *See* states, six.

realms, three (*tridhātu*)   The totality of samsara. The desire realm—so named because its inhabitants are primarily concerned with sensory gratification—includes beings of all six states of existence. The form and formless realms consist exclusively of gods whose mental states correspond with those of the eight absorption levels. The form realm corresponds to the first four absorption levels and the formless realm to the second four levels.

repa   A yogi who has activated inner heat by *tummo* yoga and thus wears only a thin cotton robe even in winter.

samsara (*saṁsāra*)   Literally "to run around"; the condition of recurrent birth through the force of action (*karma*) and afflictive mental states. It applies to all states of existence of the three realms and their six life-forms.

seed-syllable (*bīja*)   Monosyllabic mantric sounds embodying a universal principle, a deity's reality, or a psychic process.

seven superior treasures   Basic aids in all types of practice: faith, morality, modesty, receptiveness to Dharma, attentiveness, charity, and wisdom.

śāstra   The works of Indian masters that develop, systematize, or clarify the original teachings of Shakyamuni Buddha.

siddha   "Accomplished person"; one who has achieved siddhis.

siddhi   The supernormal powers developed by the practice of yoga: clairvoyance, clairaudience, levitation, thought-reading, and control of the body and external world. All siddhis are mundane (samsaric), with the exception of the supreme siddhi, enlightenment. Also, a woman siddha.

six transcendences (*pāramitā*)   Six integrated practices aimed at developing the stores of merit and gnosis: giving, morality, patience, effort, concentration, and wisdom.

Small Vehicle (*Hīnayāna*)   *See* vehicle.

social means, four (*saṃgrahavastu*)   Four practices performed by a bodhisattva primarily for the welfare of others: giving, relevant communication, assisting the development of others, and serving as an example for others.

solitary-buddha (*pratyekabuddha*)   A person of the Small Vehicle who has attained nirvana for his or her own benefit without the aid of a buddha's teachings.

states of existence, six   The six states or classes of life-forms of samsara: gods (*deva*), anti-gods (*asura*), humans (*manusya*), animals (*tiryagyona*), frustrated spirits (*preta*), and hell beings (*nairayika*). The first three are called higher states and the last three lower states.

stores, two (*saṃbhāra*)   The two accumulations of personal power: the store of merit based on ethical behavior and ritual, and the store of gnosis based on knowledge and wisdom. When completed, the two stores provide the necessary elements to achieve direct experience of voidness.

superficial reality, superficial world (*saṃvṛtisatya*)   The world as it appears when perception is conditioned by verbal conventions. The term "reality" emphasizes the fact that, owing to its relative self-consistency, it does appear to be a valid reality to ordinary beings.

supplication (*prāṇidhāna*)   Intercession with buddhas and bodhisattvas on behalf of all beings, aimed at providing for their welfare, both spiritual and temporal. "Supplication" denotes both the prayer and the mental resolution to aid beings, the latter replacing action (*karma*) and afflictive mental states in creating the rebirth and supernormal abilities of a bodhisattva.

sutra (*sūtra*) The original spoken scriptures of Shakyamuni Buddha. They are divided into three divisions or "baskets" (*piṭaka*): instruction and philosophy (*sūtra*), mental science (*abhidharma*), and discipline (*vinaya*).

tantra Scriptures of Shakyamuni and other buddhas relating to tantric, or esoteric, practice.

Tantric Vehicle (*Tantrayāna*) *See* vehicle.

three bases of practice Morality, concentration, and wisdom, which include all Buddhist practices.

three commitments (*saṃvara-śīla*) The vows of personal liberation of the Small Vehicle, the bodhisattva vows of the Great Vehicle, and the tantric vows of the Tantric Vehicle.

torma Small cakes of barley flour or other similar substances used as offerings during worship (*pūjā*).

triple gem (*triratna*) The refuge sources of Buddhism: the Buddha, representing enlightenment; the Dharma, his teachings; and the Sangha, the community of practitioners.

tummo (*caṇḍa*) The inner heat developed by one type of tantric yoga.

vajra Symbol of the indestructible and indivisible reality represented variously as a scepter, a diamond, or a thunderbolt.

Vajradhara Transhistorical buddha who is the source of the Kagyu lineage and teachings.

vajra-body (*vajrakāya*) *See* illusory-body.

vajra hell The lowest, most intense of the hells.

vehicle, three vehicles (*yāna*) The term vehicle connotes a means of traveling to enlightenment, that is, a major system of teaching and practice. The Small, or Elders', Vehicle is the oldest, relying on the scriptures set down in Pali. The Great Vehicle includes the teachings of the Small Vehicle, but in a new context and expanded scope. The Tantric Vehicle (synonym: Vajra Vehicle, Mantra

Vehicle) combines the outlook of the Great Vehicle with a radically different, high-powered system of practice.

virtues, ten (*kuśala*)   *See* evils, ten.

voidness (*śūnyatā*)   The actual nature of all things; the lack of any independent ego of persons and identity of things.

warrior (Tib. *dpa' bo*)   Male tantric figure.

white element   *See* drops.

wisdom (*prajñā*)   Generally, any correct knowledge. Specifically, transcendent wisdom, the direct perception of the void nature of persons and things. During such experience the perception of the apparent world is temporarily suppressed.

yakṣa   Destructive demons of Indian folklore.

About the Translators

LAMA KUNGA RINPOCHE, the Tibetan authority for this translation, is formerly Ngor Thartse Shabtrung of the Ngor monastery of the Sakya sect of Tibet. He is believed to be the incarnation of one of Milarepa's closest disciples. Rinpoche has been in America since the mid-1960s and currently heads Ewam Choden Dharma Center in Kensington, California.

BRIAN CUTILLO, the American translator, is a student of Geshe Wangyal and other Tibetan teachers. He also collaborated with Lama Kunga Rinpoche on the translation of additional songs and stories of Milarepa published in the volume *Miraculous Journey*.

Wisdom Publications

WISDOM PUBLICATIONS is a non-profit publisher of books on Buddhism, Tibet, and related East-West themes. We publish our titles with the appreciation of Buddhism as a living philosophy and the special commitment of preserving and transmitting important works from all the major Buddhist traditions.

If you would like more information, a copy of our mail order catalogue, or to be kept informed about our future publications, please write or call.

WISDOM PUBLICATIONS
361 Newbury Street
Boston, Massachusetts 02115
USA
Telephone: (617) 536-3358
Fax: (617) 536-1897

The Wisdom Trust

AS A NON-PROFIT publisher, Wisdom is dedicated to the publication of fine Dharma books for the benefit of all sentient beings. We depend upon sponsors in order to publish books like the one you are holding in your hand.

If you would like to make a donation to the Wisdom Trust Fund to help us continue our Dharma work, or to receive information about opportunities for planned giving, please write to our Boston office.

Thank you so much.

WISDOM PUBLICATIONS is a non-profit, charitable 501(c)(3) organization and a part of the Foundation for the Preservation of the Mahayana Tradition (FPMT).

Care of Dharma Books

DHARMA BOOKS CONTAIN THE TEACHINGS of the Buddha; they have the power to protect against lower rebirth and to point the way to liberation. Therefore, they should be treated with respect—kept off the floor and places where people sit or walk—and not stepped over. They should be covered or protected for transporting and kept in a high, clean place separate from more "mundane" materials. Other objects should not be placed on top of Dharma books and materials. Licking the fingers to turn pages is considered bad form (and negative karma). If it is necessary to dispose of Dharma materials, they should be burned with care and awareness rather than thrown in the trash. When burning Dharma texts, it is considered skillful to first recite a prayer or mantra, such as OM, AH, HUNG. Then, you can visualize the letters of the texts (to be burned) absorbing into the AH, and the AH absorbing into you. After that, you can burn the texts.

These considerations may also be kept in mind for Dharma artwork, as well as the written teachings and artwork of other religions.

Also available from Wisdom Publications

MIRACULOUS JOURNEY
New Stories and Songs by Milarepa
Translated by Lama Kunga Rinpoche
and Brian Cutillo

Miraculous Journey is a fine collection of thirty-five transcendent songs by Tibet's beloved 11th-century poet-saint, Milarepa. From advice for local villagers and nomads to his most profound precepts given to his closest disciples, Milarepa inspires and delights the reader with his insight, directness, and compassion.
Was $14.95, Now $9.95, 264 pages

THE DOOR OF LIBERATION
Essential Teachings of
the Tibetan Buddhist Tradition
Geshe Wangyal

Geshe Wangyal, a Mongolian monk and the first to teach Tibetan Buddhism in America, considered this selection of texts vital to his Western students' studies. Full of indispensable source material, this book is essential for anyone interested in Buddhism. "A mosaic of teachings that provide useful keys to liberation for the contemporary reader." —Professor Robert A.F. Thurman, Columbia University
$15.00, 264 pages

ENLIGHTENED BEINGS
Life Stories from the Ganden Oral Tradition
Janice D. Willis

Here for the first time ever in any Western language are the sacred biographies of six great tantric masters from the Gelukpa school of Tibetan Buddhism. These life stories—or *namtar*—are actually tales of liberation. Part of a distinct tradition in Tibetan Buddhism, they are meant not only to inspire but also to instruct others on the path to enlightenment.
$18.00, 318 pages

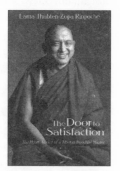

THE DOOR TO SATISFACTION
The Heart Advice of a Tibetan Buddhist Master
Lama Zopa Rinpoche

In this book, Lama Zopa Rinpoche reveals the essential meaning of an ancient thought-training text that he discovered in his retreat cave high in the Himalayas of Nepal. The message is simple: if you want to stop all problems forever and gain perfect peace of mind, you must practice the thought-training methods presented in this book. At the beginning of this teaching, Lama Zopa Rinpoche startled his audience when he declared, "Only when I read this text did I come to know what the practice of Buddhism really means."
$12.50, 182 pages